Lab Manual for Psychological Research and Statistical Analysis

Sara Miller McCune founded SAGE Publishing in 1965 to support the dissemination of usable knowledge and educate a global community. SAGE publishes more than 1000 journals and over 600 new books each year, spanning a wide range of subject areas. Our growing selection of library products includes archives, data, case studies and video. SAGE remains majority owned by our founder and after her lifetime will become owned by a charitable trust that secures the company's continued independence.

Los Angeles | London | New Delhi | Singapore | Washington DC | Melbourne

Lab Manual for Psychological Research and Statistical Analysis

Dawn M. McBride

Illinois State University

J. Cooper Cutting

Illinois State University

Los Angeles | London | New Delhi
Singapore | Washington DC | Melbourne

FOR INFORMATION:

SAGE Publications, Inc.
2455 Teller Road
Thousand Oaks, California 91320
E-mail: order@sagepub.com

SAGE Publications Ltd.
1 Oliver's Yard
55 City Road
London EC1Y 1SP
United Kingdom

SAGE Publications India Pvt. Ltd.
B 1/I 1 Mohan Cooperative Industrial Area
Mathura Road, New Delhi 110 044
India

SAGE Publications Asia-Pacific Pte. Ltd.
18 Cross Street #10-10/11/12
China Square Central
Singapore 048423

Acquisitions Editor: Abbie Rickard
Editorial Assistant: Elizabeth Cruz
Production Editor: Andrew Olson
Copy Editor: Megan Markanich
Typesetter: C&M Digitals (P) Ltd.
Proofreader: Alison Syring
Cover Designer: Candice Harman
Marketing Manager: Katherine Hepburn

Printed in the United States of America

ISBN: 978-1-5443-6349-3

This book is printed on acid-free paper.

SUSTAINABLE FORESTRY INITIATIVE
Certified Chain of Custody
At Least 10% Certified Forest Content
www.sfiprogram.org
SFI-01028

19 20 21 22 23 10 9 8 7 6 5 4 3 2 1

CONTENTS

Introduction for Instructors ix

CHAPTER 1 • Psychological Research: The Whys and Hows of the Scientific Method and Statistics 1

1a: The Purpose of Statistics 1
1b: Science in the Media 2
1c: Understanding Your Data 3
1d: Displaying Distributions 5
1e: Making and Interpreting Graphs 6
1f: Setting up Your Data in SPSS: Creating a Data File 7
1g: Displaying Distributions in SPSS 8

CHAPTER 2 • Developing a Research Question and Understanding Research Reports 9

2a: How to Read Empirical Journal Articles 9
2b: Reading Journal Articles—Mueller and Oppenheimer (2014) 12
2c: Reading Journal Articles—Roediger and Karpicke (2006) 13
2d: Reviewing the Literature 15
2e: Creating References 16
2f: APA Style 17
2g: APA-Style Manuscript Checklist 23

CHAPTER 3 • Ethical Guidelines for Psychological Research 25

3a: Ethics 25
3b: Ethics in a Published Study 27
3c: Academic Honesty Guidelines—What Is (and Isn't) Plagiarism 28
3d: Examples of Plagiarism 29
3e: Identifying and Avoiding Plagiarism 31

CHAPTER 4 • Probability and Sampling 32

4a: Distributions and Probability 32
4b: Basic Probability 34
4c: Subject Sampling 35
4d: Sampling 36

CHAPTER 5 • How Psychologists Use the Scientific Method: Data Collection Techniques and Research Designs 37

5a: Naturalistic Observation Group Activity 37
5b: Basics of Psychological Research 38
5c: Designing an Experiment Activity 40
5d: Research Design Exercise 41
5e: Design and Data Collection Exercise 42

CHAPTER 6 • Descriptive Statistics 43

6a: Central Tendency: Comparing Data Sets 43

6b: Understanding Central Tendency 44

6c: Central Tendency in SPSS 45

6d: Describing a Distribution (Calculations by Hand) 46

6e: More Describing Distributions 47

6f: Descriptive Statistics With Excel 48

6g: Measures of Variability in SPSS 49

CHAPTER 7 • Independent Variables and Validity in Research 50

7a: Identifying and Developing Hypotheses About Variables 50

7b: Independent and Dependent Variables 52

7c: Identifying Variables From Abstracts 54

7d: Identifying Variables From Empirical Articles 55

7e: Research Concepts: Designs, Validity, and Scales of Measurement 56

7f: Internal and External Validity 57

CHAPTER 8 • One-Factor Experiments 58

8a: Bias and Control Exercise 58

8b: Experimental Variables 60

8c: Experiments Exercise 61

8d: Experimental Designs 63

CHAPTER 9 • Hypothesis-Testing Logic 64

9a: Inferential Statistics Exercise 64

9b: Calculating z Scores Using SPSS 66

9c: The Normal Distribution 67

9d: z Scores and the Normal Distribution 68

9e: Hypothesis Testing With Normal Populations 69

9f: Hypothesis Testing With z Tests 70

CHAPTER 10 • t Tests 71

10a: Hypothesis Testing With a Single Sample 71

10b: One-Sample t Test in SPSS 72

10c: One-Sample t Tests by Hand 73

10d: Related-Samples t Tests 74

10e: Related-Samples t Test in SPSS 76

10f: Independent Samples t Tests 77

10g: Hypothesis Testing—Multiple Tests 78

10h: More Hypothesis Tests With Multiple Tests 79

10i: t Tests Summary Worksheet 82

10j: Choose the Correct t Test 83

10k: Writing a Results Section From SPSS Output—t Tests 84

CHAPTER 11 • One-Way Analysis of Variance 85

11a: One-Way Between-Subjects Analysis of Variance (Hand Calculations) 85

11b: One-Way Between-Subjects Analysis of Variance in SPSS 86

11c: Writing a Results Section From SPSS Output—Analysis of Variance 87

11d: Inferential Statistics and Analyses 89

CHAPTER 12 • Correlation Tests and Simple Linear Regression 91

12a: Creating and Interpreting Scatterplots 91

12b: Understanding Correlations 93

12c: Correlations and Scatterplots in SPSS 94

12d: Computing Correlations by Hand 95

12e: Hypothesis Testing With Correlation Using SPSS 96

12f: Regression 97

CHAPTER 13 • Chi-Square Tests 98

13a: Chi-Square Crosstabs Tables 98

13b: Chi-Square Hand Calculations From Crosstabs Tables 100

13c: Chi-Square in SPSS—Type in the Data 101

13d: Chi-Square in SPSS From a Data File 102

CHAPTER 14 • Multifactor Experiments and Two-Way Analysis of Variance (Chapters 14 and 15) 103

14a: Factorial Designs 103

14b: Factorial Designs Article—Sproesser, Schupp, and Renner (2014) 105

14c: Factorial Designs Article—Farmer, McKay, and Tsakiris (2014) 106

14d: Describing Main Effects and Interactions 107

14e: Factorial Analysis of Variance 108

14f: Analysis of Variance Review 109

14g: Main Effects and Interactions in Factorial Analysis of Variance 110

CHAPTER 15 • One-Way Within-Subjects Analysis of Variance 111

15a: One-Way Within-Subjects Analysis of Variance 111

15b: One-Way Within-Subjects Analysis of Variance in SPSS 112

15c: One-Way Within-Subjects Analysis of Variance Review 113

CHAPTER 16 • Meet the Formulae and Practice Computation Problems 114

16a: Meet the Formula and Practice Problems: z Score Transformation 114

16b: Meet the Formula and Practice Problems: Single-Sample z Tests and t Tests 115

16c: Meet the Formula and Practice Problems: Comparing Independent Samples and Related Samples t Tests 117

16d: Meet the Formula and Practice Problems: One-Factor Between-Subjects Analysis of Variance 119

16e: Meet the Formula and Practice Problems: Two-Factor Analysis of Variance 121

16f: Meet the Formula and Practice Problems: One-Factor Within-Subjects Analysis of Variance 124

16g: Meet the Formula and Practice Problems: Correlation 125

16h: Meet the Formula and Practice Problems: Bivariate Regression 127

Appendix A. Data Sets and Activities 128

A1: Data Analysis Exercise—von Hippel, Ronay, Baker, Kjelsaas, and Murphy (2016) 128

A2: Data Analysis Exercise—Nairne, Pandeirada, and Thompson (2008) 129

A3: Data Analysis Project—Crammed vs. Distributed Study 130

A4: Data Analysis Project—Teaching Techniques Study 131

A5: Data Analysis Project—Distracted Driving Study 132

A6: Data Analysis Project—Temperature and Air Quality Study 133

A7: Data Analysis Project—Job Type and Satisfaction Study 134

A8: Data Analysis Project—Attractive Face Recognition Study 135

A9: Data Analysis Project—Discrimination in the Workplace Study 136

Appendix B. Overview and Selection of Statistical Tests   137

    B1: Finding the Appropriate Inferential Test   137

    B2: Finding the Appropriate Inferential Test From Research Designs   138

    B3: Finding the Appropriate Inferential Test From Research Questions   139

    B4: Identifying the Design and Finding the Appropriate Inferential
    Test From Abstracts   140

    B5: Identifying Variables and Determining the Inferential Test
    From Abstracts   142

Appendix C. Summary of Formulae   144

References   147

INTRODUCTION FOR INSTRUCTORS

The *Lab Manual for Psychological Research and Statistical Analysis* is designed to allow instructors to choose from assignments that give students practice with knowledge and skills learned in a research methods and statistics course. The manual accompanies the *The Process of Research and Statistical Analysis in Psychology*, and exercises are given for each chapter of the text. The text covers the basics of research methods and statistics from a step-by-step perspective to help students learn the process of conducting research in psychology. The text also includes chapters on the statistics (descriptive and inferential) to help students properly analyze data from their own class projects. Both computations and software used in calculating statistics are covered in the text, so we have included exercises of both types (with Excel and SPSS for software) in this manual. Assignments that instructors choose not to include as required can provide students with study aids for the concepts covered. A solution key is posted on the instructor website at **http://edge.sagepub.com/mcbridermstats1e**. Chapter 16 of the manual includes Meet the Formulae sections to help students break down computational formulae for different statistics and practice the calculations involved in these formulae. Appendices include (a) analysis projects with accompanying data sets posted on the instructor and student sites for the text, (b) exercises helping students practice choosing the appropriate statistical test for a study, and (c) a summary of calculation formulas for the statistical tests.

1

PSYCHOLOGICAL RESEARCH
The Whys and Hows of the Scientific Method and Statistics

1A: THE PURPOSE OF STATISTICS

Statistics are tools that we use to understand sets of data. Consider the following fictional data set.

A	60	95		H	65	195
B	78	260		I	64	135
C	62	120		J	71	180
D	72	155		K	70	188
E	71	170		L	70	160
F	70	162		M	76	220
G	64	135		N	74	235

Assume that the data shown here are the heights (in inches) and weights (in pounds) of 14 students in a class. Answer the following questions as best as you can.

1. What does a "typical" student in this class look like in terms of height and weight?

2. Is there anyone in the class who has the same height or weight as another student? Identify any students with the same score on the two measures.

3. What are the highest and lowest weights and heights in the class? What do these values tell you about the group of students in the class?

4. How do the two different sets of measures (known as distributions) differ? Do you notice anything about these two distributions that distinguishes them?

1B: SCIENCE IN THE MEDIA

More than ever before, we are presented with data and statistics in the news. However, most of the time these analyses are reports of reports (secondary sources). In other words, they are interpreted, summarized, and often simplified by reporters. This exercise is intended to demonstrate the importance of interpreting reports as a critically informed consumer.

Part I

Instructions: Find an article in the newspaper (online newspapers are fine) that reports the results of a research finding. (*Hint:* Check the science section.)

For your chosen article, try to identify as many "scientific method details" from the research articles as you can by answering the following questions.

1. What was the title and who were the authors of the original study upon which the statements in the article are based? What was the hypothesis for the research?

2. What methodology was used (e.g., experimental, correlational, case study)? Who were the participants, and how were they recruited?

3. What were the conclusions of the research?

4. What were the limitations of the study? How convinced are you by the study's results?

5. What questions about the research do you have? What other details were left out that would be useful in evaluating the quality of the study?

Part II

Instructions: Now try to find the original research article on which the news story was based. You may be able to find the article with a search of Google Scholar, or you may need to use a research articles database (e.g., PsycINFO) to search for the original research article. Read the original article, paying close attention to the scientific method details that you summarized earlier. Then answer the following questions.

1. How well do you think the news story conveys the research findings presented in the article? (*Hint:* Read the abstract summary of the article to get a simple summary of the findings of the study.) Were the original findings accurately portrayed in the news story? Why or why not?

2. How do you think the popular press article should be changed to provide a more accurate depiction of the original research article published by the researchers?

1C: UNDERSTANDING YOUR DATA

The following table contains a data set that describes the top 25 salaries for Major League Baseball players as of opening day of the 2016 season:

Player	Team	Position	Age (as of April 28, 2016)	Salary
Kershaw	Dodgers	Pitcher	28	34.57
Greinke	Diamondbacks	Pitcher	32	34
Price	Red Sox	Pitcher	30	30
Verlander	Tigers	Pitcher	33	28
Cabrera	Tigers	First base	33	28
Hernandez	Mariners	Pitcher	30	25.85
Sabathia	Yankees	Pitcher	35	25
Lester	Cubs	Pitcher	32	25
Howard	Phillies	First base	36	25
Pujols	Angels	Designated hitter	36	25
Cano	Mariners	Second base	33	24
Hamels	Rangers	Pitcher	32	23.5
Teixeira	Yankees	First base	36	23.13
Mauer	Twins	First base	33	23
Ramirez	Red Sox	First base	32	22.75
Scherzer	Nationals	Pitcher	31	22.14
Upton	Tigers	Left field	28	22.13
Tanaka	Yankees	Pitcher	27	22
Reyes	Rockies	Shortstop	32	22
Gonzalez	Dodgers	First base	33	21.86
Crawford	Dodgers	Left field	34	21.61
Werth	Nationals	Left field	36	21.57
Ellsbury	Yankees	Center field	32	21.14
Davis	Orioles	First base	30	21.12
Shields	Padres	Pitcher	34	21

1. Who are the individuals in this data set?

2. In addition to the player's name, how many variables does the data set contain? Which of these variables take numerical values?

3. What do you think are the units in which each of the numerical values is expressed? For example, what does it mean when Howard's salary is listed as 25?

4. What is the most common position in the data set? What is the most common salary? Do you think the most common salary will be the same as the average salary? Why or why not?

1D: DISPLAYING DISTRIBUTIONS

1. Create a frequency table including the range of responses, frequency, proportion, percentage, cumulative proportion, and cumulative frequency for the following data illustrating the number of correct responses on a quiz:

   1, 4, 3, 2, 3, 4, 5, 2, 3, 5, 5, 3, 2, 1, 4, 3, 2, 3, 1, 3, 4, 3, 2, 4

2. What percentage of students scored a 3 or lower on the quiz in Question 1?

3. Create a frequency distribution graph of the data from Question 1. What is the shape of this distribution?

4. What is a typical score in the distribution? What do you know about this score in the distribution?

1E: MAKING AND INTERPRETING GRAPHS

A study has been conducted to compare men and women on the likelihood of seeking counseling for a psychological problem. A survey was completed by 1,000 men and 1,000 women to determine the number of each group suffering from anxiety or depression. The survey also asked if the respondent had sought counseling for his or her anxiety or depression. The following mean values indicate the percentage of those who reported one of the psychological problems and also sought counseling.

	Anxiety	Depression
Men	35%	15%
Women	20%	55%

1. Complete the following bar graph by including a point in the graph for each mean value given previously. Be sure to connect lines for each gender.

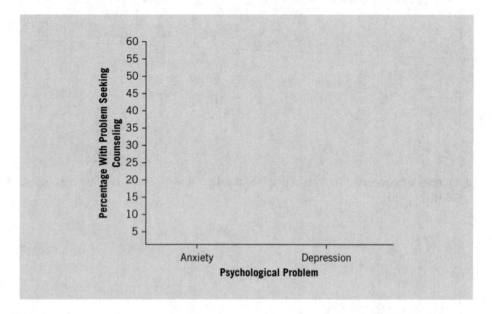

2. Re-create the graph as a bar graph using a software package such as Excel. If using Excel, type in the means and variable levels as given previously into a new worksheet, highlight what you have typed, and choose Insert Chart. Under Chart Type, you can choose a bar graph. Chart Options allow you to label the axes and adjust axis scales and fonts.

3. Describe in your own words the results displayed in the graphs.

1F: SETTING UP YOUR DATA IN SPSS: CREATING A DATA FILE

Create a data file in SPSS based on the following data, and then answer the following questions.

ID#: 568 Name: Joe Hart Age: 25 Gender: Male Income: $23,000 IQ: 105	ID#: 276 Name: Mary Swanson Age: 37 Gender: Female Income: $41,000 IQ: 115	ID#: 384 Name: Sam Lewis Age: 61 Gender: Male Income: $56,000 IQ: 125
ID#: 866 Name: Chin Lee Age: 32 Gender: Male Income: $36,000 IQ: 140	ID#: 231 Name: Al Walton Age: 39 Gender: Male Income: $29,000 IQ: 95	ID#: 476 Name: Sara Smith Age: 27 Gender: Female Income: $18,000 IQ: 90
ID#: 07 Name: David Dodge Age: 34 Gender: Male Income: $29,000 IQ: 115	ID#: 647 Name: Michelle Fried Age: 38 Gender: Female Income: $22,000 IQ: 105	ID#: 261 Name: Tom Hunt Age: 54 Gender: Male Income: $38,000 IQ: 115

1. How many individuals are in your data set? Does this match the number of rows in your SPSS data window (it should)?

2. How many variables are in your data set? Does this match the number of columns in your SPSS data window (it should)?

3. Which of your variables are categorical variables? Which are continuous variables?

4. For each variable, what measure of central tendency would you report?

1G: DISPLAYING DISTRIBUTIONS IN SPSS

Part I

Use the Datafile_1.sav data file at **http://edge.sagepub.com/mcbridermstats1e** to create a frequency distribution table for the Quiz 1 variable using SPSS. Then answer the following questions using your table.

1. What percentage of the scores is at or below a score of 7?

2. Where does it appear that most of the scores are located?

3. What does your answer to Question 2 tell you about the difficulty of the quiz?

Part II

Now create a frequency distribution table using SPSS for the second quiz variable. Compare this table to the one you created in Part I to answer the following questions.

1. For which quiz do the scores appear to be more evenly distributed across the scale?

2. Which quiz appeared to be harder? How do you know this?

DEVELOPING A RESEARCH QUESTION AND UNDERSTANDING RESEARCH REPORTS

2A: HOW TO READ EMPIRICAL JOURNAL ARTICLES

Published journal articles in psychology have a particular format that allows readers to find the information they are looking for and makes the study report clearer to the readers. Most articles will follow American Psychological Association (APA)-style guidelines, organizing the paper into the following major sections:

- Abstract
- Introduction
- Method
- Results
- Discussion
- References

We'll discuss each of the sections to familiarize you with the information you can expect to find in these sections.

Abstract

An abstract is a concise summary of the study that includes the purpose, method, main results, and conclusions of the study. The abstract must be short (under 120 words for APA style), because the abstract will be entered into the PsycINFO database to provide researchers with enough information to decide if the article is relevant to their interests. The abstract is usually the first (and possibly the only) portion of the article that a reader will encounter. It is printed at the top of the first page of the article.

Introduction

The introduction contains a lot of important information about the background and motivation for the study. A well-written introduction will begin by introducing the general topic of the study (i.e., the research question) and defining any specialized terms. The author(s) will then review what is already known about the research question by discussing past studies conducted in the area, the results found, and the relevance of each study to the current study described in the article. The author(s) will also describe the purpose or motivation for the current study, explaining why it was done and how the design used allowed them to answer the research question. In most cases, hypotheses will also be stated according to the specific results that were expected for the study.

A well-written introduction will make a clear argument for why the study is important. A reader should be able to find the argument for the study's purpose and the support provided by the author(s) in the form of a research question that has not yet been fully addressed by past studies in the topic area.

Method

The method section is a detailed description of the design and methodology of the study. It is divided into four main subsections: participants, design, materials or apparatus, and procedure. Some articles may combine some of these subsections into a single section (e.g., design and materials as one section). The goal of the method section is to allow someone to replicate the important elements of the study if they wish to do so.

Participants: This section describes the important characteristics of the participants in the study. The information should include the number of participants, important demographic information, number of participants per condition, where participants were sampled from, and compensation provided for the participants.

Design: If a separate design section is included, it will describe the variables that were manipulated and/or measured in the study. If the study is an experiment, level of the independent variables will be described and how the variables were manipulated will also be included (e.g., within subjects, between subjects).

Materials or Apparatus: The materials or apparatus section will describe the relevant materials or apparatus used for the study. Examples include specialized apparatus used for the study, computers used to present stimuli or collect responses, stimuli presented to the participants and how they were developed, questionnaires given to participants and relevant information about them, and so on. Sometimes the actual items used will be presented in an appendix that is referred to in the materials section.

Procedure: The procedure section should provide a chronological ordering of what the participants experienced during the study, including instructions for the tasks, what they saw or read, timing of presentation or task completion, what task they performed, what responses were collected from them, different conditions of the study and how participants were assigned to the conditions, and so on.

Results

The results section will include an objective report of the results found in the study. This section should include a description of the data collected and the statistical tests used to analyze the data. Summary information about the data will also be included either within the text or in tables or graphs that are referred to in the results section. Statistical test results and values will also be included in the text.

Discussion

The discussion section should review hypotheses (if they were stated in the introduction) and discuss the results in reference to the original research question. It should be clear from the discussion section what answer to the research question was provided by the study. A comparison with results of past studies will also be included, and possible explanations for discrepant or unexpected results should be provided by the author(s). The author(s) may also suggest directions for future studies in the topic area.

References

Every past study cited in the paper should be included in the references section of the article in alphabetical order. If you are researching studies in a particular area, the references section can be useful in providing leads to other relevant articles in a particular topic area. Each reference will include the authors' last names and initials in the order of authorship on the paper (this order is important; it usually indicates the order of contribution to the published article), the year the article was published, the title of the article, the journal it was published in, and the volume and page numbers of the journal.

Multiple Study or Experiment Articles

Many articles published in psychology contain more than one study or experiment. For those articles, you are likely to see a separate method and results section for each article but just one introduction and one general discussion section that tie the whole article together.

2B: READING JOURNAL ARTICLES—MUELLER AND OPPENHEIMER (2014)

This exercise accompanies a reading of the following:

Mueller, P. A., & Oppenheimer, D. M. (2014). The pen is mightier than the keyboard: Advantages of longhand over laptop notetaking. *Psychological Science, 25,* 1159–1168.

Please answer the following questions about the Mueller and Oppenheimer (2014) article (you must read through the article before you begin this assignment—the reference to the article has been provided, and the article can be found on the SAGE Student Site). For each question, indicate which section of the article (e.g., introduction, method) the information was in.

1. State the research question.

2. Discuss some of the past research regarding hand note taking versus laptop note taking. Which is more advantageous to learning? (*Hint:* All researchers may not agree.)

3. Do the researchers state a specific hypothesis? If so, what is it? If not, what is your hypothesis (or prediction)?

4. Study 1: How did the researchers design the experiment to answer their research question? (This can be found in the method section.)

5. What change in methodology did the researchers make from Study 1 to Study 2? Why?

6. Was the change (from Question 5) effective in answering their follow-up question?

7. What were some possible limitations of Study 2, and how did they design Study 3 to alleviate those limitations?

8. Briefly summarize the main (and important) findings from Study 1, Study 2, and Study 3.

9. Overall, what do the results suggest for note taking?

10. What are some real-world applications of this study, and how can students use this information for their own learning?

2C: READING JOURNAL ARTICLES— ROEDIGER AND KARPICKE (2006)

This exercise accompanies a reading of the following:

Roediger, H. L., III, & Karpicke, J. D. (2006). Test-enhanced learning: Taking memory tests improves long-term retention. *Psychological Science, 17,* 249–255.

Please answer the following questions about the Roediger and Karpicke (2006) article (you must read through the article before you begin this assignment—the reference to the article is provided, and the article can be found on the SAGE Student Site).

1. The research question addressed in this study is this:
   a. Of all study techniques, which is the best?
   b. Which study technique do students use most often?
   c. Which study technique is better: rereading or recalling?
   d. Which information is better remembered: a story about otters or a story about the sun?

2. The researchers' hypothesis in this study is this:
   a. Information about otters will be remembered better than information about the sun.
   b. Recalling information will result in better memory than rereading the information.
   c. Rereading information will result in better memory than recalling information.
   d. None of the above.

3. Learning condition in Experiment 1 was manipulated within subjects. This means that _____.
   a. all subjects received both the rereading and recalling learning conditions
   b. subjects only completed either the rereading or the recalling learning condition
   c. subjects did not receive either of these conditions in the study

4. The main results of Experiment 1 were that _____.
   a. recall for the otter passage was higher than recall for the sun passage
   b. recall was higher when subjects recalled the passage than when they reread the passage before the final test for all test delays
   c. subjects recalled more about the passage they found more interesting
   d. recall was higher when subjects recalled the passage than when they reread the passage before the final test—but only for test delays greater than 5 min

5. Experiment 2 was conducted to _____.
   a. replicate the results of Experiment 1
   b. generalize the results of Experiment 1 to new passages
   c. examine effects of taking multiple tests between study and the final test
   d. both a and c

6. The results of Experiment 2 showed that _____.
   a. recalling the passages always resulted in better memory than rereading them
   b. repeated tests of the passages resulted in less forgetting over the 1-week delay than the other learning conditions
   c. subjects recalled less information when the passages were changed

7. The primary conclusion from this study is that _____.
   a. people remember more about animals than other topics
   b. recalling information will help you remember better than rereading it over the long term
   c. the best study technique for students seems to be rereading their notes
   d. all of the above

2D: REVIEWING THE LITERATURE

1. How does an empirical journal article differ from a popular magazine article (e.g., an article in *Time* magazine)? Who is the intended audience of empirical journal articles in psychology?

   An empirical journal article is written to describe a research study, address a research question, publish data and explain the study's results. They are primary sources and intended for anyone interested in the topic, especially other researchers looking for background on a particular topic. This differs from a popular magazine article because they contain shorter summaries, may not give an accurate account of the data, and are secondary sources.

2. Describe how you might use PsycINFO to conduct a literature review on the topic of obesity stereotypes and biases. Describe the steps you would take to collect relevant articles for your literature review and what you might expect to find at each step.

3. Using PsycINFO, find an article authored by Larry L. Jacoby that was published in 1991, and then write the APA-style reference for the article.

4. Using PsycINFO, find a recent article (2014–2019) that examines the relationship between violence on TV and violent behavior in children. Write the APA-style reference for the article.

5. You've probably heard the saying "opposites attract." This is really a hypothesis about what people are attracted to, and research in psychology has attempted to test this hypothesis. For this exercise, you will search for studies that tested this hypothesis. However, before you begin, you must first convert the saying into a research question about behavior.

   a. State the research question for this saying in terms of behavior that might be examined in a research study.

   b. Using your research question to develop keywords (do NOT type in the saying), conduct a literature search using PsycINFO to find one article that provides empirical evidence that either supports or does not support the hypothesis. In your own words, write a paragraph indicating why you think the article supports or does not support the hypothesis. Attach a copy of the abstract of the article, and describe how you conducted your search.

   c. Describe how the empirical evidence you found could be used by companies that run dating sites (e.g., match.com) to help their clients identify potential dating partners.

2E: CREATING REFERENCES

For the following PsycINFO references, retype each one in APA style.

1. Voss, Joel L; Paller, Ken A. Neural correlates of conceptual implicit memory and their contamination of putative neural correlates of explicit memory. [References]. [Journal; Peer Reviewed Journal] Learning & Memory. Vol 14(1–6) Jan-Jun 2007, 259–267. Year of Publication 2007

2. Carnagey, Nicholas L; Anderson, Craig A; Bushman, Brad J. The effect of video game violence on physiological desensitization to real-life violence. [References]. [Journal; Peer Reviewed Journal] Journal of Experimental Social Psychology. Vol 43(3) May 2007, –496. Year of Publication 2007

3. Blass, Thomas. Understanding behavior in the Milgram obedience experiment: The role of personality, situations, and their interactions. [References]. [Journal; Peer Reviewed Journal] Journal of Personality and Social Psychology. Vol 60(3) Mar 1991, 398–413. Year of Publication 1991

4. Wagman, Jeffrey B; Malek, Eric A. Perception of Whether an Object Can Be Carried Through an Aperture Depends on Anticipated Speed. [References]. [Journal; Peer Reviewed Journal] Experimental Psychology. Vol 54(1) 2007, 54–61. Year of Publication 2007

5. Meyers, Adena B; Landau, Steven. Best Practices in School-Based Sexuality Education and Pregnancy Prevention. [References]. [Book; Edited Book] Thomas, Alex (Ed); Grimes, Jeff (Ed). (2002). Best practices in school psychology IV (Vol. 1, Vol. 2). (pp. 1523–1536). xv, 909 pp. Washington, DC, US: National Association of School Psychologists. Year of Publication 2002

6. McDaniel, Mark A; Einstein, Gilles O. Spontaneous Retrieval in Prospective Memory. [References]. [Book; Edited Book] Nairne, James S (Ed). (2007). The foundations of remembering: Essays in honor of Henry L. Roediger, III. (pp. 225–240). xi, 451 pp. New York, NY, US: Psychology Press. Year of Publication 2007

2F: APA STYLE

Identify as many APA-style errors as you can find in the following short paper.

The Survival Affect

In Free Recall

RUNNING HEAD: Survival Affect

Abstract

Memory for words studied in three different contexts was examined. In one study context, subjects rated items for their importance in surviving in the wilderness. In another context, subjects rated items for their importance in moving to another country. Finally, in the 3rd context, subjects rated the pleasantness of a list of items. Subjects then recalled the items in the list. Subjects were tested individually in a small lab room that measured 8 feet by 11 feet. Free recall results were very significant. Thus, the authors concluded that the survival affect is real. Further experiments confirmed this.

Introduction

We tested whether items studied in a survival context are better remembered than items studied in other contexts. Previous studies (like Nairne et al., 2007) have suggested that a survival context can improve memory. These results support the proposal that memory developed to aid human survival. The current study tested this.

Method

Subjects

Students from a psychology course volunteered. There were twenty-three of them. It was for course credit. Three came on a Monday and the rest came on a Thursday. Some were assigned to each context condition.

Materials

The experiment occurred in a small lab room with white walls. The floor had gray carpeting.

Subjects were tested individually in front of a computer. The experimenter told the subject that they would be rating items presented on the screen and then the instructions for one of the study contexts (survival, moving, pleasantness) were presented on the screen.

The items presented came from a norming study conducted in 2004 (Van Overschelde, Rawson, & Dunlosky). Each participant saw 44 items and rated each one according to the instructions. After the rating task, subjects were given a blank sheet of paper (8.5 inches by 11 inches) and asked to write down as many of the items as they remembered.

Procedure

Most of the procedure is described above. Items were presented for 4 seconds each in the rating task. Subjects were given 2 minutes to recall all the items in the list.

Results

Table 1. The results were very significant. A statistical test showed that F was 6.78. This was a p less than .05 so our hypothesis was right. The means were 60% for survival, 52% for moving, and 53% for pleasantness. This shows that memory is important for survival.

Discussion

The experiment was designed well. We know this because our results showed significance. This tells us that experiencing things in a survival context can help our memory. This further proves that the purpose of memory is to help us survive. Future experiments can help prove this as well.

Table 1 Mean Percentage of Items Recalled as a Function of Study Context

Study Context	Mean
Survival	60
Moving	52
Pleasantness	53

References

James S. Nairne, Sarah R, Thompson, and Josefa N. S. Pandeirada, (2007). Adaptive Memory: Survival Processing Enhances Retention. *Journal of Experimental Psychology: Learning, Memory and Cognition,* Volume 33, No. 2, pgs. 263-273.

2G: APA-STYLE MANUSCRIPT CHECKLIST

Title Page

- Title
- Author(s)
- Affiliation(s)
- Running head
- Page number

Abstract

- Statement of the issue
- Brief hypothesis
- Brief description of the method
- Brief description of the results and conclusions

Introduction

- Problem of interest
- Link between problem and past research
- Summary of past research
- Description of the basic purpose of the current experiment
- Description of the hypotheses (conceptual-level independent variable and dependent variable)

Method

- Thorough description of the study
- Participant description
- Design—Independent variables and dependent variables, operational definitions
- Materials—Description of the stimuli
- Procedure—How the experiment was performed

Results

- Descriptive statistics
- What inferential statistics were used; what alpha level
- Results of the statistical analyses

Discussion

- Hypotheses that were supported or rejected
- Implications of the results

- Possible alternative explanations
- Future directions

References

- Are all the appropriate references cited?
- Are all the references cited in the text?
- Are the citations in the appropriate APA format?

Tables and Figures

- Each figure on a separate page
- Figures are clear and neat
- Tables follow APA-style guidelines
- Tables and figures cited in text

Writing

- Overall clarity
- Grammar
- Spelling
- APA format

3

ETHICAL GUIDELINES FOR PSYCHOLOGICAL RESEARCH

3A: ETHICS

Pretend that you are a member of the institutional review board (IRB). Read each of the following research proposals, and evaluate the study for adherence to ethical principles of research conduct. Think about and answer the following questions to help you evaluate each study. Make suggestions, where possible, on how to improve the study to meet ethical guidelines.

1. Does the study have scientific merit? How will society or the subjects of the study benefit?

2. Does the study place subjects at risk for either physical or psychological harm? If it does, what aspects of the study cause this risk? Can you suggest less risky procedures that would still provide the researcher with the same information?

3. Will subjects read and sign a consent form? If not, is there enough information given to the subjects to provide informed consent?

4. Does the study use deception? If it does, will the subjects be fully debriefed? Can you think of a way for the researchers to answer the research question without using deception?

5. Can the participants reasonably refuse to participate or withdraw during the study? If not, what part of the study appears to be coercive?

6. Will the subjects' data be kept confidential?

7. Do you have any other concerns about the study? If so, what are they?

Study 1: The current study will examine the idea that exercise will interfere with performance in an attention task. In the experiment, participants will be strapped to a treadmill while they also respond verbally to images on a computer screen. The experimenter will control the speed of the treadmill during the experiment. The participant will also be told that the experiment takes 1 hr and that they will receive $250 if they successfully complete the experiment. All participants will sign a consent form if they wish to participate. To avoid distractions during the experiment, the participants will run in a soundproof room, and no communication between the participants and the experimenter will be allowed after the experiment has started. However, as a safety precaution, the experimenter will continuously monitor the participants' heart rates. After the participant is given instructions, the participant will be strapped to a restraining device that is connected to the treadmill. The participants' task will be to respond to target stimuli by verbally identifying the objects presented. The participants will be fully debriefed after the experiment.

Study 2: This study will examine conflict resolution behaviors between romantic couples. Participants will be romantic couples who have been dating for 6 months or more. They will be asked to separately fill out questions about personal topics (e.g., sexual behaviors, drug and alcohol behaviors). Then the couple will be placed in a room together and asked to talk about an issue in their relationship. The session will be videotaped and later coded for conflict resolution behaviors by the experimenter. To be able to match the questionnaires with the tapes of the sessions, participants will be asked to put their name on the questionnaires when they complete them.

Study 3: In order to test the effects of control of eating behaviors on stress responses, rats will be run in pairs through an experiment. One rat in the pair will be presented with food whenever it makes the correct response in a discrimination task. A second rat will be presented with food at random times (i.e., not connected to its behavior). The rats and their food will be visible to each other during the experiment. Immediately after the experimental session, the rats will be removed from the test chambers and sacrificed. Their stomachs will be inspected for ulcers. The study will determine if the rats that lack control over the availability of food develop more stomach ulcers than the other rats. This information may have implications for the health of humans with different eating habits. Therefore, the important information this study will provide justifies the use of shock treatments to the animals.

Study 4: In a simulation training study, undergraduate participants will be asked to help another participant learn a list of words. In reality, though, the participant learning the words will be an experimenter confederate who purposely gets some of the words wrong. The actual participants will be told that they have to scold the learner whenever the learner makes a mistake.

Any time the participants hesitate in scolding the learner for mistakes, the experimenter will tell them that they must scold the learner or they will not receive credit for the experiment. The number of times the participants scold the learners will be recorded. Each participant will sign a consent form before the experiment begins.

3B: ETHICS IN A PUBLISHED STUDY

Download and read the following article (the article is available on the SAGE Student Site):

Cantlon, J. F., & Brannon, E. M. (2006). Shared system for ordering small and large numbers in monkeys and humans. *Psychological Science, 17,* 401–406.

In response to the article, please respond to the following questions:

1. Summarize the research question, the basic procedure used, and the results of the research.

2. What ethical issues did the researchers need to address for the human participants in this study?

3. What ethical issues did the researchers need to address for the nonhuman subjects in this study?

4. Even though all of the participants were in the same study (Experiment 2), the researchers face different ethical issues with the two groups. Compare and contrast the ethical issues of the two groups of participants.

3C: ACADEMIC HONESTY GUIDELINES— WHAT IS (AND ISN'T) PLAGIARISM

When you are working on reporting research (either that you conducted or that others conducted that you are summarizing), it is especially important that you understand the ethical guidelines regarding academic honesty. Here are some guidelines as they apply to writing about research:

1. When writing a journal article summary, it will be necessary to use some of the terms in the article. However, the assignment is a summary of the article to be written in your own words. Do not quote from the article (quotes do not "summarize"), and do not use more than five words in succession from the article or you will be plagiarizing the authors. A good way to prepare to write a summary is to make notes in your own words as you read the article, and then write from your notes instead of from the article itself. Reordering words in a sentence someone else has written also constitutes plagiarism.

2. American Psychological Association (APA)-style papers require you to cite background sources (this means to indicate the authors and year of publication in parentheses when you get info from a source—it doesn't mean you can copy word for word from a source). You may not use more than five words in succession written by someone else in your paper unless you identify this material as a direct quote (by using quotation marks), and for most assignments, you will not be allowed to quote. If you are simply discussing what others reported in their written reports (without quoting), you must cite the authors when you begin the discussion. See the APA manual for proper formatting of citations.

3D: EXAMPLES OF PLAGIARISM

The following paragraphs provide examples of three commonly used forms of plagiarism. Read through each paragraph and the explanations of the plagiarism examples. Then rewrite the original paragraph in your own words without plagiarizing the paragraph.

Original Paragraph

Author: Dawn McBride, 2006.

A patient known only as H. M. suffers from a particular form of amnesia. At the age of 27, H. M. had surgery to decrease the symptoms of his epilepsy. During the surgery, an area near the center of his brain called the hippocampus was damaged. The hippocampus aids in the storage of new memories. When H. M. awoke from the surgery, he could remember facts about himself and episodes from his life before the surgery, but he could not remember new people he met or new facts about the world or himself. In other words, H. M. has anterograde amnesia; since his surgery, he has not been able to create new memories that last longer than a few minutes. His condition keeps him from living a normal life.

Verbatim Plagiarism

Amnesia is a medical condition that has been found to impair an individual's ability to remember information. There is more than one type of amnesia that can affect an individual.

A patient known only as H. M. suffers from a particular form of amnesia. At the age of 27, H. M. had surgery to decrease the symptoms of his epilepsy. When the surgery was being performed, **an area near the center of his brain called the hippocampus was damaged. The hippocampus aids in the storage of new memories.** Upon awakening from the surgery, **he could remember facts about himself and episodes from his life before the surgery, but he could not remember new people he met or new facts about the world or himself. In other words, H. M. has anterograde amnesia; since his surgery, he has not been able to create new memories that last longer than a few minutes.** This unfortunate affliction limits the daily activities that H. M. is capable of engaging in.

Comments

The words highlighted in **bold** were written exactly as they appeared in the original passage.

This is considered plagiarism, as the author of the rewritten passage has made no attempts to use quotation marks to indicate that the words were not his or her own. In addition, the author provides no citation for the work from which this information was taken. Although the entire passage has not been lifted from the original work, the author is still required to provide quotation marks and a citation.

Lifting Selected Passages

Amnesia is a medical condition that has been found to impair an individual's ability to remember information. There is more than one type of amnesia that can affect an individual.

A patient known only as H. M. was affected by *a particular form of amnesia.* The treatment that H. M. underwent *to decrease the symptoms of his epilepsy* involved extensive surgical procedures wherein a section of his brain was removed to reduce the erratic electrical brain activity that was causing the seizures. During the procedure, *an area near the center of his brain* was damaged beyond repair. As a result, H. M. was no longer able to form new memories.

Although H. M. could not form new memories, he could still *remember facts about himself and episodes from his life before the surgery.* This type of amnesia is called anterograde amnesia.

This condition has precluded H. M. *from living a normal life.*

Comments

These paragraphs display the author's attempt to paraphrase the original passage while lifting only select passages from the original. This is still considered plagiarism, as the author used *five or more words in a row* from the original passage in several places without providing a citation or quotation marks. This type of plagiarism can be avoided by using quotation marks around the lifted passages and providing citations or by paraphrasing the lifted passages using his or her own words and providing a citation of the source.

Paraphrasing the Structure of the Paragraph Without Citations

An individual who was known in the medical community as H. M. was diagnosed with a specific type of amnesia. In order to reduce the number of seizures H. M. experienced as a result of his epilepsy, he underwent brain surgery when he was 27. When surgeons removed the afflicted areas of the brain, damage was caused to an area of the brain known as the hippocampus. Research has revealed that the primary function of the hippocampus is the formation of new memories. Upon awakening, H. M. found himself unable to store any new information regarding specific events and personal experiences. This type of amnesia is known as anterograde amnesia. H. M.'s memories that existed before the surgery remain preserved, whereas information encoded after the surgery is highly transient. This condition imposed severe limitations on the type and amount of daily activities that H. M. could complete without the assistance of others.

Comments

In this paragraph, the author did not lift any passages from the original paragraph. However, this paragraph has the same structure as the original, and there are no citations. This is the most common type of plagiarism found. This type of plagiarism can be prevented by simply citing the source. For example, this paragraph could begin with a statement of who the original author was along with an indication that the following paragraph would be a restatement of the original author's words. In addition, the citation could come at the end of the paragraph if the author chooses.

3E: IDENTIFYING AND AVOIDING PLAGIARISM

Consider the abstract from the following source:

Lane, L. W., Groisman, M., & Ferreira, V. S. (2006). Don't talk about pink elephants! Speakers' control over leaking private information during language production. *Psychological Science, 17,* 273–277.

Abstract

Speakers' descriptions sometimes inappropriately refer to information known only to them, thereby "leaking" knowledge of that private information. We evaluated whether speakers can explicitly control such leakage in light of its communicative consequences. Speakers described mutually known objects (e.g., a triangle) that had size-contrasting matches that were privileged to the speakers (e.g., a larger triangle visible to the speakers only), so that use of a contrasting adjective (e.g., small) involved referring to the privileged information. Half the time, speakers were instructed to conceal the identity of the privileged object. If speakers can control their leaked references to privileged information, this conceal instruction should make such references less likely. Surprisingly, the conceal instruction caused speakers to refer to privileged objects more than they did in the baseline condition. Thus, not only do speakers have difficulty not leaking privileged information, but attempts to avoid such leakage only make it more likely.

1. Write a summary of the abstract that uses three different kinds of plagiarism (as discussed in Exercise 3d).

2. Rewrite your summary without using any plagiarism.

4 PROBABILITY AND SAMPLING

4A: DISTRIBUTIONS AND PROBABILITY

1. Use the study description and data set that follows to create a frequency distribution table:

    Assume you are interested in people's ability to regulate their actions. You administer the temporal discounting measure (TDM) to 25 Introductory Psychology students and record their scores. Scores seen in past samples range from 10 to 20. The students' raw scores are shown here:

    11, 12, 13, 18, 12, 12, 17, 10, 15, 14, 17, 16, 14, 14, 15, 19, 11, 13, 20, 12, 14, 15, 12, 13, 16

2. Once you have created your frequency distribution table, use it to answer these questions:

    a. Does it look to you as if this sample is scoring similar to those other samples?

    b. Does it appear that this sample has a majority of high-scoring individuals (closer to 20) or low-scoring individuals (closer to 10)?

    c. Do you see scores that look abnormal or outside the range of most other scores?

3. Imagine that a population is made up of numbered marbles in a bag and that your task is to reach in and pull out one marble. Use the following frequency distribution table and graph for this population to answer the following questions.

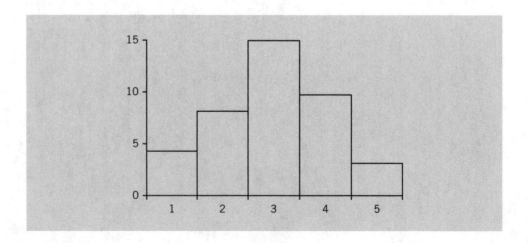

X	f	p
5	2	.05
4	10	.25
3	16	.40
2	8	.20
1	4	.10

a. What is the probability of selecting (sampling) a marble with a 3 on it?

b. What is the probability of selecting (sampling) a marble with a 5 on it?

c. What is the probability of selecting a marble with a value greater than 2?

d. What is the probability of selecting a marble with a value less than 5?

e. What is the probability of selecting a marble with a value greater than 1 and less than 4?

4B: BASIC PROBABILITY

Consider the following populations and samples. For each, try to decide which population the sample was more likely to have been drawn from.

1. A standard deck (we'll call it Population 1) has 52 cards: one card for numbers 2 through 10 and a jack, queen, king, and ace for each of the four suits (♥, ♦, ♣, ♠).

    A pinochle deck (we'll call it Population 2) has 48 cards: one card for numbers 2 through 8 and two for 9 through ace (9, 10, jack, queen, king, ace) for each of the four suits (♥, ♦, ♣, ♠).

    If you were dealt 9♥, 10♠, J♣, K♠, A♥ (our sample), which deck (population) is this hand more likely to have come from? Explain your answer. How certain do you feel about your choice?

2. At the local game store, you pick up two 6-sided dice. One die is a true die: the chances of rolling a 1, 2, 3, 4, 5, or 6 are all equivalent. The other die is a loaded die that has been weighted so that the 1 happens very infrequently, the 6 occurs more frequently than usual, and the 2, 3, 4, and 5 occur at their normal rates. The two dice look the same, and you forget which is which. You decide to pick one of them and roll it six times (our sample). Suppose that your sample roll is 1, 1, 3, 2, 6, 2. Which die do you think you selected: the true die or the loaded die? Explain your answer. How certain do you feel about your choice?

4C: SUBJECT SAMPLING

1. Find a report about a poll from a newspaper or the Internet (e.g., http://people-press.org), and summarize the main findings.

2. Discuss how the respondents were sampled.

3. Discuss the strengths and potential weaknesses of the sampling method used in the study.

4. How is your interpretation of the results affected by the sampling method used?

4D: SAMPLING

1. Your college wants to gather student opinion about parking for students on campus. It isn't practical to contact all students.

    a. Design a bad sample. Give an example of a way to choose a sample of students that is poor practice because it depends on voluntary response.

    b. Design another bad sample. Give an example of a way to choose a sample of students that is poor practice that doesn't involve voluntary response.

    c. Design a good sample. Give an example of a way to choose a sample of students that is good practice.

2. Suppose that a university club has 25 student (S) members and 10 faculty (F) members. Their names are as follows:

Barrett	S	Duncan	S	Hu	S	Lee	S	Reeder	F
Bergner	F	Frazier	S	Jarvis	F	Main	S	Ren	S
Brady	S	Gibellato	S	Jimenez	S	McBride	F	Santos	S
Chen	S	Gulati	S	Kahn	F	Nemeth	S	Sroka	S
Critchfield	F	Han	S	Katsaounis	S	O'Rourke	S	Tobin	F
DeSouza	F	Hostetler	S	Kim	S	Paul	S	Tordoff	S
Draper	S	House	F	Kohlschmidt	S	Pryor	F	Wang	S

Assume that the club may send only one person to an international conference.

    a. What are the odds of sending Dr. Kahn to the conference?

    b. What are the odds of sending a student to the conference?

    c. What are the odds of sending somebody with the last name that begins with the letter *K*?

5

HOW PSYCHOLOGISTS USE THE SCIENTIFIC METHOD

Data Collection Techniques and Research Designs

5A: NATURALISTIC OBSERVATION GROUP ACTIVITY

Instructions: Choose one of the following research questions to study. Then follow the steps in the Research Procedures section to conduct your study.

Research Questions

1. Do people walking alone walk faster than people walking in groups of two or more?

2. Which campus building has more traffic (i.e., people going in and out) between classes?

3. Do more males or females hang out on the quad between classes?

4. Which entrance to the student center is used most often between classes?

Research Procedures

1. As a group, discuss your research question and decide on a reasonable predicted answer to your research question. Be sure to record WHY you think this is the answer you will obtain.

2. As a group, discuss ways to use naturalistic observation of people on campus to answer your research question. Be sure to decide on the following:

   a. How long you will observe your subjects (no longer than 20 min)

   b. How you will observe the subjects UNOBTRUSIVELY

   c. What you will observe or measure

   d. How your observations will answer your research question (i.e., What observations do you expect if your prediction is correct?)

   e. Identifying your subject or independent variable and your dependent variable(s)

3. Conduct your study and collect your observations.

4. Discuss what you found in your observations and how you would answer your research question based on those observations.

5. Prepare and present the following to the class:

   a. Your research question and prediction (including why you made that prediction)

   b. Your variables (identify whether you have a subject or independent variable and your dependent variable)

   c. Your method (how you obtained your observations)

   d. The answer to your research question from your observations

   e. Any limitations you found using this method to answer your question

6. Briefly discuss what worked well and what didn't work well with your naturalistic observation. If you had it to do all over again, what would you do differently? Why?

5B: BASICS OF PSYCHOLOGICAL RESEARCH

Short-Answer Questions

1. Give an operational definition for *hungry*.

2. Give an example of a hypothesis that can be made from the theory "sleeplessness causes depression."

3. What is the difference between a data-driven hypothesis and a theory-driven hypothesis?

4. What is the purpose of conducting a literature review when conducting a research study?

5. In what ways does naturalistic observation differ from other data collection techniques?

Multiple-Choice Questions

6. Psychologists use which method of knowing in learning about behavior?
   a. logic
   b. authority
   c. observation
   d. intuition

7. Which of the following is NOT a key element of an experiment?
   a. control
   b. an independent variable
   c. naturalistic observation
   d. causal explanations

8. The best synonym for a theory is _____.
   a. a prediction
   b. an explanation
   c. a bias
   d. an independent variable

Use the following description to answer questions 9 through 11. A study was conducted to learn about the social interactions of elementary-aged schoolchildren. The children were observed during recess for a 6-month time period. Results showed that as age of the children increased, they were more likely to have verbal interactions with their peers.

9. The study described is an example of the _____ research method.
   a. experimental
   b. naturalistic
   c. case study
   d. correlational

10. The study described employs the use of which data collection method?
    a. archival data
    b. naturalistic observation
    c. experimental data
    d. interviews

11. Which of the following was a dependent variable in the study?
    a. age
    b. observation time
    c. social interaction
    d. a and c
    e. b and c
    f. none of the above

12. In which section of a journal article would you find a listing of the raw data?
    a. introduction
    b. method
    c. results
    d. none of the above

5C: DESIGNING AN EXPERIMENT ACTIVITY

Complete this exercise in a small group:

Your group's task is to choose an issue that follows (or one assigned to your group by your instructor) and design an experiment (or series of experiments if you deem it necessary) to examine it.

- Does watching violence on TV cause violent behavior?

- Does playing video games improve hand–eye coordination in other tasks?

- Does smoking cause lung cancer?

- Does studying with background music improve test scores?

- Does living in a large city decrease helping behaviors?

- Does color affect mood?

- Does caffeine affect work productivity?

Be sure to include information about what your variables are, how you will manipulate your independent variables, how you will measure your dependent variables, what control conditions you need, who your participants are, etc. Make sure that you give enough thought and detailed discussion to all of these issues to design a good study to answer the question.

1. Individually, provide a description of the experiment that your group designed (including the information mentioned previously).

2. Now spend some time evaluating the experiment that your group designed. You should consider the adequacy of the following:
   - The way the dependent variable(s) is/are measured
   - The way the independent variable(s) is/are manipulated
   - If there are enough appropriate control conditions
   - What, if any, threats there are to internal and external validity
   - What potential confounds there are
   - How you would describe the design of your experiment

5D: RESEARCH DESIGN EXERCISE

For the research questions that follow, design a study to answer the question using the research design specified. Be sure to describe any variables you would include in the study as well as any operational definitions needed.

1. Does watching violence on TV cause violent behavior? (experiment)

2. Do people who play video games have better hand–eye coordination in other tasks? (correlational)

3. Does divorce in families negatively affect children? (case study)

4. Are smoking and lung cancer related? (quasi-experiment)

5. Does studying with background music improve test scores? (experiment)

6. Are there fewer helping behaviors in large cities? (correlational)

7. Are color and mood related? (correlational)

8. Are caffeine and work productivity related? (quasi-experiment)

9. Does watching violence on TV cause violent behavior? (correlational)

10. Do people who play video games have better hand–eye coordination in other tasks? (experiment)

5E: DESIGN AND DATA COLLECTION EXERCISE

For each study description that follows, identify the data collection technique and the research design that were used.

1. Researchers (Bartecchi et al., 2006) were interested in the effects of a new law banning smoking in public places on health. They compared heart attack rates for two cities of comparable size where one city had enacted a smoking ban 1 year before the study and the other city had no smoking ban. To compare heart attack rates, the researchers examine hospital records for the hospitals in each city. They compared heart attack rates for the year before the smoking ban in each city and for the year after the ban was enacted. They found that heart attack rates decreased in the city with the ban from 1 year to the next but did not decrease in the city without the ban.

    Data Collection Technique:

    Research Design:

2. To evaluate the validity of a newly created survey measure of college students' satisfaction with their major, a researcher (Nauta, 2007) administered the survey to college students who had declared a major. She then also collected the students' grade point averages (GPAs; with their permission) from the university registrar to examine the relationship between their survey score and their GPA. She found that satisfaction with major was positively correlated with GPA.

    Data Collection Techniques (There is more than one in this study.):

    Research Design:

    What does it mean that she found a positive relationship between GPA and survey score?

3. Researchers (Assefi & Garry, 2003) were interested in the effects of the belief that one has consumed alcohol on cognition. In particular, they tested whether a belief that subjects had consumed alcohol during the study would increase their susceptibility to memory errors. Subjects were randomly assigned to one of two groups. In one group they were told the drink they consumed had contained alcohol (with some alcohol rubbed on the outside of the glass for realism). In the other group, they were told the drink did not contain alcohol. All subjects then saw a slide show of a crime (shoplifting). After a short delay, subjects then read a description of the crime that contained errors. After another short delay, they answered questions about the slides they had seen and were asked to rate their confidence in their answers. Subjects told they drank alcohol made more errors in their answers and were more confident in their responses.

    Data Collection Technique:

    Research Design:

6

DESCRIPTIVE STATISTICS

6A: CENTRAL TENDENCY: COMPARING DATA SETS

For each data set that follows, calculate the mean, median, and mode. Then answer the questions that follow.

1. Data Set 1: 21, 22, 23, 24, 24, 24, 25, 25, 25, 25, 26, 27, 28
   a. *Mean:*

   b. *Median:*

   c. *Mode:*

2. Data Set 2: 20, 20, 20, 21, 21, 21, 21, 21, 27, 27, 28, 28, 28, 28
   a. *Mean:*

   b. *Median:*

   c. *Mode:*

3. Which data set has the highest mean?

4. Is the mean the best measure of central tendency for these two distributions? Why or why not?

6B: UNDERSTANDING CENTRAL TENDENCY

1. What is the value of the mean, median, and mode for the following set of scores?

   Scores: 1, 3, 5, 0, 1, 3

2. In a sample of $n = 6$, five individuals all have a score of 10, and the sixth person has a score of 16. What is the mean for this sample?

3. After 5 points are added to every score in a distribution, the mean is calculated and found to be 30. What was the value of the mean for the original distribution?

4. For a perfectly symmetrical distribution with mean = 30, what is the value of the median?

5. For the following set of scores, identify which measure would provide the best description of central tendency and explain your answer.

   Scores: 0, 30, 31, 33, 33, 34, 35, 37, 38

6C: CENTRAL TENDENCY IN SPSS

For this exercise, use the downloadable Datafile_1.sav data file at **http://edge.sagepub.com/ mcbridermstats1e.**

1. Using SPSS for your computations, answer the following questions.
    a. What is the mean for the final variable?

    b. What is the median for the final variable?

    c. What is the mode for the final variable?

    d. What percentage of students scored lower than the mode on the final?

    (*Hints:* Don't include the students who scored the mode exactly. Don't include % in your answer. Round to 1 digit. Thus, 22.2% would be entered as 22.2.)

2. Look at the distribution in the following histogram to answer the questions.
    a. From lowest to highest, list the mean, median, and mode.
    b. Of the three measures of central tendency (mean, median, and mode), which is the least representative number for this distribution?
    c. Which type of skew (positive or negative) is evident in this distribution?

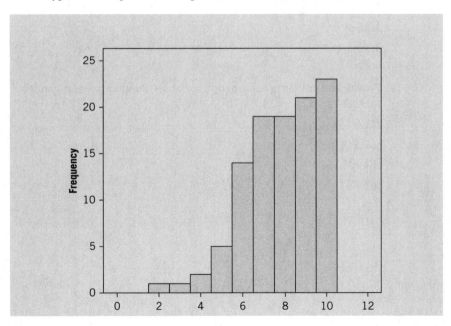

6D: DESCRIBING A DISTRIBUTION (CALCULATIONS BY HAND)

Suppose that you conducted a survey examining how much your friends ($n = 10$) like a "how to study" website and if their rating of the site is related to their grade point average (GPA). Your survey's response scale runs from 0 = *not like at all* to 5 = *absolutely love*. Your sample of 10 has these results for the survey (X): 5, 1, 2, 4, 3, 2, 4, 3, 0, 3.

Display results in a frequency distribution table and a histogram.

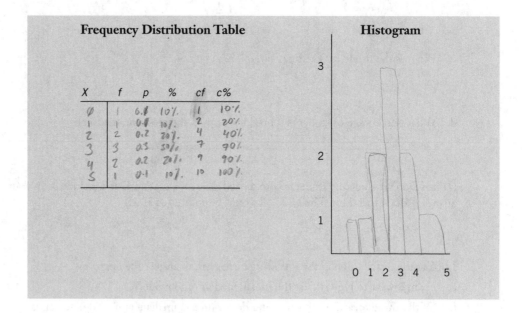

X	f	p	%	cf	c%
0	1	0.1	10%	1	10%
1	1	0.1	10%	2	20%
2	2	0.2	20%	4	40%
3	3	0.3	30%	7	70%
4	2	0.2	20%	9	90%
5	1	0.1	10%	10	100%

a. Find measures of central tendency for the sample:
   Mean: 2.7
   Median: 3
   Mode: 3

b. Provide the following information about the sample (where p stands for "probability of"):
   $p(X = 3) = 0.3$
   $p(X > 0) = 0.9$
   $p(0 < X < 4) = 0.6$
   $p(X > 4) = 0.1$

6E: MORE DESCRIBING DISTRIBUTIONS

1. In a population of $N = 10$ scores, the smallest score is $X = 8$ and the largest score is $X = 20$. The range of the population is __12__.

   $20 - 8 = 12$

2. A sample of $n = 5$ scores, the mean is 20 and $s^2 = 4$. What is the sample standard deviation?

   sample std dev = 5 $\sqrt{s^2} = s$ $\sqrt{4} = 2$

3. A population of scores has a mean of 50 and standard deviation of 12. If you subtract five points from every score in the population, then the value of the new standard deviation will be __12__.

4. What is the value of the sum of squares for the following scores?
   Scores: 1, 1, 1, 3

   mean = 1.5 $(1 - 1.5)^2 \times 3 + (3 - 1.5)^2 = 3$

5. Compute the sum of squares, variance, and standard deviation for the following population of scores.
   Scores: 9, 1, 8, 6

   mean = 6 $(9 - 6)^2 + (1 - 6)^2 + (8 - 6)^2 + (6 - 6)^2 = 38 = SS$

   variance $= \frac{38}{4} = 9.5$

   std dev $= \sqrt{9.5} = 3.08$

6F: DESCRIPTIVE STATISTICS WITH EXCEL

One widely available program for calculating descriptive statistics is Microsoft's Excel. Excel is a spreadsheet program that can be used by researchers to manage and analyze data sets. The following exercise is designed to introduce you to some of the basic descriptive statistical resources within Excel that may be useful in your course.

Use the data listed in the table and Excel to compute the means and standard deviations for each condition.

	A	B
1	Control	Treatment
2	45	64
3	65	76
4	75	83
5	56	69
6	46	66

6G: MEASURES OF VARIABILITY IN SPSS

1. Open Datafile_1.sav data file at **http://edge.sagepub.com/mcbridermstats1e.** Use this file and SPSS to answer these questions:

   a. What are the mean, standard deviation, and range for Quizzes 1 through 5?

   b. Which quiz has the largest variability based on range? Based on standard deviation?

2. Consider the following three distributions of data:

Distribution 1	Distribution 2	Distribution 3
1, 2, 3, 3, 4, 4, 4, 5, 5, 5, 5, 5, 6, 6, 6, 7, 7, 8, 9, 9	3, 3, 3, 3, 4, 4, 4, 5, 5, 5, 5, 5, 6, 6, 6, 7, 7, 7, 7, 8	1, 3, 3, 4, 4, 5, 5, 5, 5, 5, 5, 5, 5, 6, 6, 6, 7, 7, 9

   Type the data from the three distributions into a new file in SPSS.

   a. Just looking at the numbers, for which distribution is variability the lowest? Why did you come to that conclusion?

   b. For each distribution, use SPSS to construct a histogram, compute the range, and find the standard deviation.

   c. Which measure of variability is most affected by extreme values? (*Hint:* Compare the second and third distributions.)

INDEPENDENT VARIABLES AND VALIDITY IN RESEARCH

7A: IDENTIFYING AND DEVELOPING HYPOTHESES ABOUT VARIABLES

Finding and developing research ideas takes practice. One source of some research ideas is our common wisdom. This exercise provides practice developing commonly held beliefs into testable research ideas. Listed here are 10 statements that are common clichés (many of which you may have heard at some point in your life). Pick two of the clichés, and turn them into testable research ideas, following the example provided here.

Absence makes the heart grow fonder.	Experience is the best teacher.
All work and no play make Jack a very dull boy.	An apple never falls far from the tree.
Good fences make good neighbors.	He who laughs last laughs longest.
Ignorance is bliss.	A rose by any other name still smells as sweet.
Opposites attract (relationships).	An apple a day keeps the doctor away.

For each of the clichés that you select, please do the following:

- Identify a potential research method that may be used to investigate the idea.

- Identify the relevant variables, and specify how the researcher might manipulate and/or measure the variables.

- Identify other variables that might be relevant (e.g., to control or measure).

Example: Laughter is the best medicine.

Research Method: Experiment

Independent Variable: Laughter condition
This variable may be operationalized by manipulating whether there is laughter present or absent.

Dependent Variables: "Best Medicine"—this probably could refer to many different variables that we consider "health."

This variable may be operationalized by measuring a variety of aspects of health:

- Physiological health may be measured with a standard physical examination by a physician.

- Psychological health may be measured with a set of questionnaires designed to measure aspects of psychological health.

Other Potentially Relevant Variables: "Medicine" suggests that "laughter" is a treatment for an ailment, so factors like the type and severity of the ailment might be important variables to measure or control.

7B: INDEPENDENT AND DEPENDENT VARIABLES

Part I. Identifying Independent Variables and Dependent Variables

Remember that an independent variable is manipulated, while a dependent variable is measured and may change as a result of exposure to the independent variable.

1. Jury decisions are influenced by the attractiveness of the defendant.

    Independent Variable:

    Dependent Variable:

2. A drug company is advertising a new drug that helps people recover from jet lag faster. You are skeptical, so you conduct an experiment to test their claim. In your experiment, 100 people are flown from San Francisco to Tokyo. During the flight, half the participants are given the drug company's new drug. The other half of the participants are given a placebo (i.e., sugar pill) during the flight. Six hours after they land, all participants are asked to rate how sleepy and disoriented they feel.

    Independent Variable:

    Dependent Variable:

3. Vohs and Schooler (2008) conducted a study to investigate the effect of beliefs about free will on behavior. Thirty college students participated in their study. Participants were randomly assigned to read one of two paragraphs taken from the same book. One of the paragraphs suggested that scientists believe that free will is an illusion. The other paragraph discussed consciousness and did not mention the topic of free will. All participants were then asked to complete a set of math problems, presented one at a time on a computer screen. Participants were asked to complete each problem. They were also told that the computer program had an error such that the answers to some of the problems may appear with the problem and that they should try to solve the problems on their own (they could make the answer disappear by pressing the space bar when the problem appeared). The researchers measured the number of times the participants pressed the space bar as a measure of cheating behavior (more presses equals less cheating).

    Independent Variable:

    Dependent Variable:

Part II. Operationally Defining Variables

Remember that the variables we make hypotheses about are often abstract constructs. Designing research to examine the relationships between variables involves the process of operationally defining those variables in terms of how they are manipulated or measured. Consider each of the following research descriptions: (a) identify the variables, and (b) briefly describe how they are operationally defined.

4. The nonconscious mimicry of the behaviors of interacting partners is referred to as the chameleon effect. Chartrand and Bargh (1999) performed a study to examine how mimicry within an interaction influenced the quality of the interaction and liking between partners. They had pairs of participants describe what they saw in photographs. One of the participants in each pair was a confederate (working with the researchers). Half of the confederates were instructed to mirror the behaviors of their partner, while the other half engaged in neutral mannerisms. Following the picture description interaction, participants completed questionnaires asking them to report how much they liked their partner (the confederate) and how smoothly the interaction had gone. The results showed that participants rated the interaction smoother and reported liking their partners more in the mimic condition than in the neutral condition.

5. These days, advertising is a nearly omnipresent part of our lives. While we may be consciously aware of the obvious attempts of advertisers to influence our behaviors, we may not be aware of more subtle effects. Braun and Loftus (1998) conducted research in which they investigated how memories about an object (already experienced) can change as a function of advertising (presented after experiencing the object). In their first experiment, the researchers demonstrated that memories can be altered by presentation of misleading information in advertisements. Their follow-up experiment examined whether this effect would persist if people knew that the advertisements may contain misleading information. In this study, participants believed that they were participating in a chocolate taste test experiment. They were presented samples of the candy in a green wrapper, and they tasted and rated the product. Following a brief filler task, respondents were asked to evaluate advertisements for the product. The advertisement presented misleading information about the color of the wrapper (suggesting that the wrapper was blue). Following another brief filler task, participants were given a memory test for the color of the wrapper used in the taste test by selecting the color from a color wheel. The researchers also told the participants that some of the colors in the advertisement were not representative of the true colors. Some participants were told this when they saw the advertisements; others were told only at the memory test. The researchers again found a strong misinformation effect of the advertisement despite the explicit warnings given to participants. The effect was strongest when the warning was given at the memory test. The authors concluded that warning consumers about past misleading advertising may have little effect because the misinformation may have already become incorporated into memory.

7C: IDENTIFYING VARIABLES FROM ABSTRACTS

1. Find the abstract for each of the following articles (either in PsycINFO or in the journal):

   a. Stanley, M. L., Henne, P., & De Brigard, F. (in press). Remembering moral and immoral actions in constructing the self. *Memory and Cognition.*

   b. Abel, M., & Roediger, H. L., III (2018). The testing effect in a social setting: Does retrieval practice benefit a listener? *Journal of Experimental Psychology: Applied, 24*(3), 347–359.

   c. Axt, J. R. (2018). The best way to measure explicit racial attitudes is to ask about them. *Social Psychological and Personality Science, 9*(8), 896–906.

2. Print a copy of these abstracts with your lab exercise.

3. Try to identify as many of the following as possible from each abstract:

   a. the participants (e.g., kids, college students)

   b. independent and dependent variables

   c. main results

   d. implications of the results

7D: IDENTIFYING VARIABLES FROM EMPIRICAL ARTICLES

This exercise accompanies a reading of the article that follows (available on the SAGE Student Site):

Sayette, M. A., Reichle, E. D., & Schooler, J. W. (2009). Lost in the sauce: The effects of alcohol on mind wandering. *Psychological Science, 20,* 747–752.

Please answer the following questions about the variables used in the Sayette et al. (2009) study (you will need to read the article to answer most of the questions).

1. The purpose of the Sayette et al. (2009) study was to investigate the effect of alcohol on mind wandering (i.e., lapses of attention to a task). Based on the purpose and title of the article (and without reading the article), what do you think the independent and dependent variables in this study were?

    Independent Variable:

    Dependent Variable:

2. After reading the article, can you state the authors' research question using the conditions in their study?

3. What was the primary independent variable in the study? How was it manipulated (i.e., what was the researchers' operational definition of *alcohol*)?

4. What were the dependent variables in the study (i.e., how did the researchers operationally define *mind wandering*)? How were they measured?

5. What results were found in a comparison of the independent variable groups for each dependent variable? In other words, for which dependent variables were there group differences, and which group had a higher mean score on each dependent variable?

6. Overall, what did the authors learn from this study?

7E: RESEARCH CONCEPTS: DESIGNS, VALIDITY, AND SCALES OF MEASUREMENT

1. Does regular exercise reduce the risk of a heart attack? Here are two ways to answer this question:

   Study 1: A researcher finds 2,000 men over age 40 who exercise regularly and have not had heart attacks. She matches each with a similar man who does not exercise regularly, and she follows both groups for 5 years.

   Study 2: Another researcher finds 4,000 men over age 40 who have not had heart attacks and are willing to participate in a study. He assigns 2,000 of the men to a regular program of supervised exercise. The other 2,000 continue their usual habits. The researcher follows both groups for 5 years.

   a. Explain why the first is an observational (i.e., not an experimental) study and the second is an experiment.

   b. Why does the experiment give more useful information about whether exercise reduces the risk of heart attacks?

2. A researcher evaluates a new growth hormone. One sample of rats is raised with the hormone in their diet, and a second sample is raised without the hormone. After 6 months, the researcher weighs each rat to determine whether the rats in one group are significantly larger than the rats in the other group.

   A second researcher measures femininity for each individual in a group of 10-year-old girls who are all daughters of mothers who work outside of the home. These scores are then compared with corresponding measurements obtained from girls who are all daughters of mothers who work at home. The researcher hopes to show that one group is significantly more feminine than the other.

   What issues with internal and external validity do you think might apply to this study?

3. Identify the scale of measurement (nominal, ordinal, interval, or ratio) that leads to each of the following conclusions:

   a. Peter's score is larger than Phil's, but we cannot say how much larger.

   b. Peter's score is 3 times larger than Phil's.

   c. Peter and Phil have different scores, but we cannot say which one is larger, and we cannot determine how much difference there is.

7F: INTERNAL AND EXTERNAL VALIDITY

For each abstract that follows, evaluate the internal and external validity of the study (remember, in many studies, the higher one is, the lower the other is). Also, identify two or three issues that could threaten the internal validity of the study.

1. There is evidence suggesting that children's play with spatial toys (e.g., puzzles and blocks) correlates with spatial development. Females play less with spatial toys than do males, which arguably accounts for males' spatial advantages; children with high socioeconomic status (SES) also show an advantage, though SES-related differences in spatial play have been less studied than gender-related differences. Using a large, nationally representative sample from the standardization study of the Wechsler Preschool and Primary Scale of Intelligence–Fourth Edition and controlling for other cognitive abilities, we observed a specific relation between parent-reported frequency of spatial play and block design scores that was invariant across gender and SES. Reported spatial play was higher for boys than for girls, but controlling for spatial play did not eliminate boys' relative advantage on this subtest. SES groups did not differ in reported frequency of spatial play. Future research should consider quality as well as quantity of play and should explore underlying mechanisms to evaluate causality (Jirout & Newcombe, 2015).

2. Although self-rated personality traits predict mortality risk, no study has examined whether one's friends can perceive personality characteristics that predict one's mortality risk. Moreover, it is unclear whether observers' reports (compared with self-reports) provide better or unique information concerning the personal characteristics that result in longer and healthier lives. To test whether friends' reports of personality predict mortality risk, we used data from a 75-year longitudinal study (the Kelly/Connolly Longitudinal Study on Personality and Aging). In that study, 600 participants were observed beginning in 1935 through 1938, when they were in their mid-20s, and continuing through 2013. Male participants seen by their friends as more conscientious and open lived longer, whereas friend-rated emotional stability and agreeableness were protective for women. Friends' ratings were better predictors of longevity than were self-reports of personality—in part because friends' ratings could be aggregated to provide a more reliable assessment. Our findings demonstrate the utility of observers' reports in the study of health and provide insights concerning the pathways by which personality traits influence health (Jackson, Connolly, Garrison, Leveille, & Connolly, 2015).

3. We showed that anticipatory cognitive control could be unconsciously instantiated through subliminal cues that predicted enhanced future control needs. In task-switching experiments, one of three subliminal cues preceded each trial. Participants had no conscious experience or knowledge of these cues, but their performance was significantly improved on switch trials after cues that predicted task switches (but not particular tasks). This utilization of subliminal information was flexible and adapted to a change in cues predicting task switches and occurred only when switch trials were difficult and effortful. When cues were consciously visible, participants were unable to discern their relevance and could not use them to enhance switch performance. Our results show that unconscious cognition can implicitly use subliminal information in a goal-directed manner for anticipatory control, and they also suggest that subliminal representations may be more conducive to certain forms of associative learning (Farooqui & Manly, 2015).

8

ONE-FACTOR EXPERIMENTS

8A: BIAS AND CONTROL EXERCISE

For each study description that follows, list possible confounding variables that might be present in the study based on the description provided.

1. A researcher wanted to determine whether different forms of exercise improve memory and problem-solving skills—with the hope of helping treat elderly people with cognitive impairments. She recruited 10 members of the swim team and 10 members of the track team at a local college to be tested on two types of tasks. Each group received a memory task that involved memorizing a list of 10 words and recalling them as well as a problem-solving task that involved solving anagrams of these same 10 words (an anagram is a jumbled word that needs to be rearranged, like HBCEA for BEACH). The swim team received the memory task followed by the problem-solving task, and the track team received the problem-solving task followed by the memory task. Each group was tested 15 min after its respective team practices (either swim or track). The results showed a significant interaction in that members of the swim team performed significantly better on the problem-solving task than the track team, and the members of the track team performed significantly better on the memory task than the swim team members. The researcher concluded that to help elderly people with their problem-solving skills, they should swim more, and to help with their memory, elderly people should take up running or jogging.

2. Tsapelas, Aron, and Orbuch (2009) recently conducted a study to examine the effects of boredom on marital satisfaction. Participants included 123 couples. Couples were questioned separately in their homes after 7 years of marriage and after 16 years of marriage. At each session, couples were asked to rate how much they felt their marriage was "in a rut" and how satisfied they were with their marriage. Results of the study indicated that boredom with marriage at 7 years was related to a decrease in marital satisfaction at 16 years.

3. A social psychologist is interested in studying the effect of the size of a group on problem solving. She conducts the experiment in her two Introductory Psychology courses. During a class exercise in each class, she asks students to form groups of two, five, or eight to work on the activity. She records how quickly each group finishes the task. She conducts related samples t tests to compare the completion times for the three group sizes. She finds that groups of two finished faster than the other two groups, and groups of size five finished faster than groups of eight.

For each description that follows, read the description of the study and then answer the questions about the sources of bias and how to control for them.

4. I want to conduct an experiment to determine the effect of instructional mode on learning. I have students learn material either in a computer-based interactive environment or by reading a traditional text. One group of students gets the computer-based instruction, and the other group reads the text. Both groups are presented with the same material and spend the same amount of time learning the material. Both groups are given the same test at the completion of learning. I find that the group with the computer-based instruction scores higher on the final test. However, I have a confound of previous knowledge of the students in my experiment, so my results are not valid. Think of a few different ways I can redesign my experiment to control for this confounding.

5. I have designed an experiment to learn how attention processes operate in search tasks. I present participants with a display that contains letters placed in random positions on a computer screen. The participants' task is to find a colored X among a field of other letters. Participants are to report the color of the X when they find it on the screen. I am interested in how the shapes of the distractors (the other letters) affect the speed of the task. To determine this, I first run participants through a set of 50 trials where all of the distractors are rounded letters (such as O and Q) and then I run them through a set of 50 trials where all of the distractors contain straight lines (such as T and K). For the rounded distractors, I use Xs that are blue, red, or yellow. For straight-line distractors, I use Xs that are green, brown, or orange. I have a set of similar participants (education, visual abilities, etc.), and I have controlled for the number of each type of letter serving as a distractor. The presentation timing of all trials is exactly the same. I find that participants are slower on the trials with straight-line letters as distractors. I have two major confounds in this experiment, which makes my data invalid. One is the order in which the participants are given the two letter conditions. What is the other? How can I redesign my experiment to control for these sources of bias?

8B: EXPERIMENTAL VARIABLES

1. Dr. Jacobs conducts a research study investigating the effects of a new drug that is intended to reduce the craving for alcohol. A group of alcoholics who are being treated at a clinic is selected for the study. One half of the participants are given the drug along with their regular treatment, and the other half receives a placebo. After 6 months, Dr. Jacobs records how many days each individual has gone without consuming alcohol.

   a. Identify the independent variable in this study.

   b. Identify the number of levels (and what they are) of the independent variable.

   c. Identify the dependent variable of the experiment.

   d. Assuming that the study includes participants in age from 18 to 62 years of age, what kind of variable is age?

   e. If the participants in the drug group are noticeably older than those in the placebo group, what might this do to the data? In this case, what type of variable is age in the study?

2. In an experiment, participants are usually assigned to treatments using a random assignment procedure. Explain why random assignment is used.

3. A researcher wants to know if brighter lights make factory workers more productive. Workers in a factory are randomly assigned to two groups. One group is moved to a new factory next door where the factory lights are brighter. The other group stays behind in the old factory. The productivity of the two groups is compared.
   a. Identify the independent variable(s).
   b. Identify the dependent variable(s).
   c. What is a plausible confounding variable in this study?

4. A researcher wants to know if it helps patients if their therapists disclose personal information about themselves. Participants are randomly assigned to one of two groups. One group has therapists who previously have indicated that they tend to disclose a lot about themselves in therapy. The other group has therapists who previously have indicated that they rarely disclose personal information in therapy.
   a. Identify the independent (or explanatory) variable(s).
   b. Identify the dependent (or response) variable(s).
   c. What is a plausible confounding variable in this study?

8C: EXPERIMENTAL EXERCISE

Part I. Introduction

Imagine that you were a participant in an experiment where you were asked to eat cookies and rate how much you liked each cookie on a scale from 1 to 5, where higher ratings mean higher liking of the cookie. You are asked to eat an Oreo cookie and rate it and then eat a Chips Ahoy cookie and rate it. For this experiment, answer the following questions.

1. What is the independent variable? What are the levels of the independent variable?

2. Was the independent variable manipulated between subjects or within subjects? How do you know?

3. What is the dependent variable? What operational definition was used in this experiment?

4. What scale of measurement was used for the dependent variable?

5. The independent variable was bivalent. Explain how you can make it multivalent.

6. Change the cookie experiment into a factorial experiment. Explain what you would need to add and what conditions you would have in your factorial experiment.

7. Do you think the cookie experiment has more internal validity or external validity? Explain your answer.

Part II. Testing Causal Relationships— Roediger and Karpicke (2006)

One question students often ask is how they can best prepare for exams in their classes. This is a question that we can answer based on experiments. For example, some researchers (e.g., Roediger & Karpicke, 2006) wanted to know if reading over your notes is an effective way to remember information for a test. But they wanted to test the causal link between study method and memory, so they compared two learning conditions for text material (e.g., a passage about sea otters) in an experiment to see which of the study conditions resulted in better memory performance. In one condition, subjects read through the passage and then tried to recall what they read without rereading it. In the other condition, subjects read through the passage and then reread the passage a few times for the same amount of time that the other group spent recalling the passage. Thus, this study compared techniques like reading over your notes or reading chapters that are reported fairly often with techniques like quizzing yourself and teaching to someone else, which are reported less frequently (see the graph on the next page for some sample data that students might report when asked what study techniques they use in preparing for exams). Both groups of subjects in the study took a final recall test on the passage after a delay. They found that after 2 days (let's pretend you all study for an exam 2 days before it instead of the night before), the read–test group recalled almost 70% of the passage ideas, and the read–read group recalled only about 52% of the passage ideas. Use this study description to answer the questions that follow.

8. What is the independent variable in the Roediger and Karpicke (2006) study? What are the levels? How does this independent variable connect with real-world situations?

9. What was their dependent variable? How was it operationally defined?

10. Why does the Roediger and Karpicke (2006) study show that the read–test study technique *causes* one to remember better? Why doesn't the sample survey data that follows show that the read over your notes technique listed most often *causes* better test scores?

Sample Data From Class Survey on Study Techniques

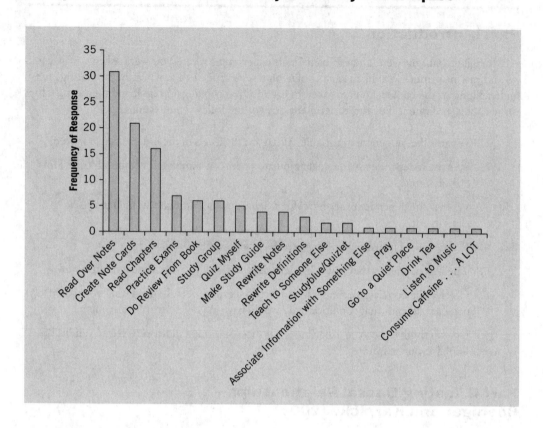

8D: EXPERIMENTAL DESIGNS

1. A psychologist is interested in the effect of peer pressure on risk-taking behaviors of college students. The psychologist designs an experiment to determine this effect where 200 students (who volunteer to serve as participants) are randomly placed in one of two situations. In each situation, five participants sit in a room with four other people. The four other people are actually confederates of the experimenter (i.e., they are part of the experiment), and their behavior is determined before the experiment begins. Half of the participants witness the four other people in the room leaning back in their chairs (a behavior that involves the minor risk of falling over backward in the chair). The other half of the participants also witness the four confederates leaning back in their chairs but are further encouraged by the confederates to exhibit the same behavior (e.g., they tell the subjects that leaning back is more comfortable, fun). The behavior of each participant is observed to determine whether he or she does or does not lean back in the chair during the experiment. For each group, the number of participants (out of five) who lean back in their chairs is recorded.

   a. List any independent variables in this study and the levels of each one.

   b. What is the dependent variable, and how is it being measured?

   c. What type of experimental design is this (e.g., bivalent, multivalent, or factorial)?

2. Explain why an experiment typically has higher internal validity but lower external validity than other research methods.

3. A research methods instructor wants to know if having students conduct their own research study as part of the course increases their understanding of major concepts in the course. To investigate this, she gives two sections of her course a pretest on the course concepts. She then gives one section a research study assignment for the course but does not give this assignment to her other section. At the end of the semester, she gives a posttest to both sections on the course concepts and compares the difference in the pretest–posttest scores as a measure of learning for the two sections of her course. The section with the research study assignment shows more learning. Explain why the instructor cannot be sure that the research study assignment *caused* more learning in this study.

9

HYPOTHESIS-TESTING LOGIC

9A: INFERENTIAL STATISTICS EXERCISE

Part I. Making Hypotheses

For each study that follows, state the null hypothesis. Then review the results for the study and decide what your decision (accept or reject) should be with regard to the two hypotheses (null and alternative). Remember, you should NEVER accept a null hypothesis.

Study 1

Alternative Hypothesis: Anxiety increases lying in children.

a. *Null Hypothesis:*

   Study 1 Results: A study compared 50 children who were placed in an anxiety-inducing situation with 50 children in a control group. They were then asked about their behavior, and the number of inaccurate responses was recorded. Inaccurate responses did not differ for the two groups.

b. We should _____ the null hypothesis.

c. We should _____ the scientific hypothesis.

d. Suppose that the study was conducted inaccurately and that anxious children really do lie more. In this case, we have made a **Type I Type II** (circle one) decision error.

Study 2

Alternative Hypothesis: People are more likely to help a stranger if there is no one else around than if they are in a group (i.e., the bystander effect).

a. *Null Hypothesis:*

   Study 2 Results: A situation was set up on a busy highway where someone needed help with her car. Researchers observed 100 cars drive by and counted the number of people who stopped and whether they were alone or with other people in the car. People driving with others stopped less often to help than people who were driving alone.

b. We should _____ the null hypothesis.

c. We should _____ the scientific hypothesis.

d. Suppose that the study contains a confounding variable, and when tested properly, people driving with others actually stop just as often as people driving alone. In this case, the study described above has led us to make a **Type I Type II** (circle one) decision error.

e. Whenever we reject the null hypothesis, what does this tell us about the independent variable?

Part II. Inferential Statistics

Study 3

A behavioral psychologist conducts an experiment to determine whether operant conditioning techniques can be used to improve balance in people who consider themselves "clumsy." She recruits 50 participants—each of whom responds yes to the question "Do you consider yourself clumsy?" on a preexperimental questionnaire. Half the participants are given a balance task (stand on one foot with your arms in the air) with the time they can balance recorded. They are then excused and asked to return 3 weeks later. The other half of the participants are given 3 weeks of operant training during a balance exercise. In this training, the participants are asked to perform the balance task just described. Each time they can beat their previous balance time, they receive $10. After the 3-week period, all participants are asked to perform the balance task again. Alpha is set at .05. The members of the training group can balance for an average of 25 s. Members of the control group (who did not receive the training) can balance for an average of 24.3 s. When the inferential statistical test is conducted on these data, $p = .08$.

1. What is the independent variable for this study? The dependent variable?

2. What is the alternative hypothesis?

3. What is the null hypothesis?

4. What *population* is being tested in this study?

5. Is the difference observed in the study statistically significant? Why or why not?

6. Based on your answer to Question 5, what decision should be made about the null hypothesis?

7. In the context of this experiment, what *exactly* is p the probability of?

Study 4

Some have claimed that children of divorced parents are not as well adjusted as children of parents who are married. To test this idea, you set up a study with two groups. One group consists of 100 children who have divorced parents. The other group consists of 100 children who have married parents. Each child in the study is asked to complete the Social Adjustment Scale for Children (SASC). Higher scores on the scale indicate better social adjustment.

1. Does this study contain an independent variable? Why or why not?

2. What dependent variable is measured in this study?

3. What is the null hypothesis for this study?

4. What is the alternative hypothesis?

The results indicate a mean difference of 10 on the SASC scale between the two groups of children—with alpha set at .05, $p = .02$.

5. What decision should be made with regard to the null hypothesis?

6. Describe one possible source of bias that could be present in this study causing the results that were observed.

9B: CALCULATING *z* SCORES USING SPSS

1. Open the datafile Datafile_2.sav at **http://edge.sagepub.com/mcbridermstats1e** in SPSS. Plot a histogram of SAT Math scores of the students in this file (satm).

2. Convert every score in the distribution (SAT Math) to a *z* score with SPSS.

   a. Using SPSS to make a histogram of the new zsatm variable, what does it look like (what is the shape)? How does it compare to the original satm histogram?

   b. What is the mean and standard deviation? Explain why we get these values for the mean and standard deviation (think about the *z* score formula).

Using Standard Scores to Compare Different Distributions

Consider the following two standardized distributions.

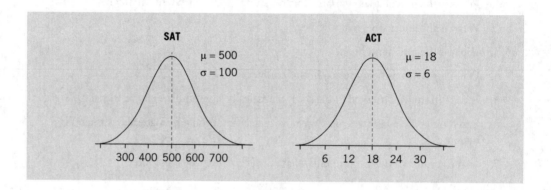

3. Suppose that you got a 540 on the SAT and a 20 on the ACT for the distributions described previously. Which score is better?

4. Suppose instead that you got a 600 on the SAT and a 24 on the ACT. Now which score is better?

9C: THE NORMAL DISTRIBUTION

1. Answer the following questions about the normal distribution:

   a. What percentage of the area under the curve is between the mean and the rightmost end of the curve?

   b. What percentage of the area under the curve is within one standard deviation of the mean (on either side of the mean)?

2. Using the unit normal table, determine the following:

   a. Find the probabilities that correspond to the following z scores: 2.0, 0.5, −0.75, −2.0

   b. Find the z scores that correspond to the following probabilities: 0.5000, 0.8413, 0.3050

3. Assume that the following is true: The scale for the SAT is set so that the distribution of scores is approximately normal with mean = 500 and standard deviation = 100.

   a. What is the probability of having an IQ of 130 or above?

   b. What is the probability of having an IQ of 120 or above?

   c. What is the probability of having an IQ score of 91 or less?

   d. You think that you might need a tutor. You know of a tutoring service for students who score between 350 and 650 on the SAT. You think that you probably fit within their range. What is the probability that you will get an SAT score between 350 and 650?

   e. The National Collegiate Athletic Association (NCAA) requires Division I athletes to score at least 820 on the combined mathematics and verbal parts of the SAT exam in order to compete in their first college year. In 1999, the scores of the millions of students taking the SATs were approximately normal with a mean = 1017 and a standard deviation = 209. What is the probability of scoring an 820 or less in this distribution?

9D: z SCORES AND THE NORMAL DISTRIBUTION

Use the following means and standard deviations:

ACT, $\mu = 21, \sigma = 3$

SAT, $\mu = 500, \sigma = 100$

1. You take the ACT test and the SAT test. You get a 24 on the ACT and a 660 on the SAT. The college that you apply to needs only one score. Which do you want to send them (i.e., Which score is better: 24 or 660?). Why?

2. What is the probability of having an ACT score of 20 or less?

3. What SAT score do you need to have to be in the top 15% of the population?

4. What is the probability of scoring between 500 and 650 on the SAT?

5. What is your percentile rank if you have an ACT of 25.5?

9E: HYPOTHESIS TESTING WITH NORMAL POPULATIONS

1. Each of the following situations calls for a significance test of a population mean. State the null hypothesis H_0 and the alternative hypothesis H_a in each case.

   a. The diameter of a spindle in a small motor is supposed to be 5 mm. If the spindle is either too small or too large, the motor will not work properly. The manufacturer measures the diameter in a sample of motors to determine whether the mean diameter has moved away from the target.

   b. U.S. Census Bureau data show that the mean household income in the area served by a shopping mall is $52,500 per year. A market research firm questions shoppers at the mall. The researchers suspect the mean household income of mall shoppers is higher than that of the general population.

   c. The examinations in a large psychology class are scaled after grading so that the mean score is 50. The professor thinks that one teaching assistant is a poor teacher and suspects that his students have a lower mean than the class as a whole. The teaching assistant's students this semester can be considered a sample from the population of all students in the course, so the professor compares their mean score with 50.

2. A researcher would like to test the effectiveness of a newly developed growth hormone. The researcher knows that under normal circumstances laboratory rats reach an average weight of 1,000 g at 10 weeks of age. When the sample of 10 rats is weighed at 10 weeks, they weigh 1,010 g.

   a. Assuming that the growth hormone has no effect, what would a Type I error be in this situation?

   b. Assuming that the growth hormone does have an effect, what would a Type II error be in this situation?

9F: HYPOTHESIS TESTING WITH z TESTS

1. Suppose we think that listening to classical music will affect the amount of time it takes a person to fall asleep, so we conduct a study to test this idea.

   a. Suppose that the average person in the population falls asleep in 15 min (without listening to classical music) with $\sigma = 6$ min. State the null and alternative hypotheses for this study.

   b. Assume that the amount of time it takes people in the population to fall asleep is normally distributed. In the study, we have a sample of people listen to classical music, and then we measure how long it takes them to fall asleep. Suppose the sample of 36 people fall asleep in 12 min. What is the probability of obtaining a sample mean of 12 min or smaller? Assuming $\alpha = .05$, is your calculated p value in the critical region? (*Hint*: Remember to consider two critical regions.)

   c. Using your answer Question b, what decision should be made about the null hypothesis you stated in Question a?

   d. Assume now that in reality classical music does not affect how long it takes people to fall asleep. In this case, what kind of decision (correct, Type I error, or Type II error) have you made in Question c?

2. A psychologist examined the effect of chronic alcohol abuse on memory. In this study, a standardized memory test was used. Scores on this test for the general population form a normal distribution with $\mu = 50$ and $\sigma = 6$. A sample of $n = 22$ alcohol abusers had a mean score of $X = 47$. Is there evidence for memory impairment among alcoholics? Use $\alpha = .05$ for a one-tailed test. Write out each step of hypothesis testing.

3. On a vocational interest inventory that measures interest in several categories, a very large standardization group of adults (i.e., a population) has an average score of $\mu = 22$ and $\sigma = 4$. Scores are normally distributed. A researcher would like to determine if scientists differ from the general population in terms of writing interests. A random sample of scientists is selected from the directory of a national science society. The scientists are given the inventory, and their test scores on the literary scale are as follows: 21, 20, 23, 28, 30, 24, 23, 19. Do scientists differ from the general population in their writing interests? Test at the .05 level of significance for two tails. Write out each step of hypothesis testing.

10

t TESTS

10A: HYPOTHESIS TESTING WITH A SINGLE SAMPLE

Consider the following scenarios. For each, determine which formula (*z* or *t*) is appropriate to use to answer the question asked. (You don't need to do any computations.)

1. Pat, a personal trainer, would like to examine the effects of humidity on exercise behavior. It is known that the average person in the United States exercises an average of $\mu = 21$ min each day. The personal trainer selects a random sample of $n = 100$ people and places them in a controlled atmosphere environment where the relative humidity is maintained at 90%. The daily amount of time spent exercising for the sample averages 18.7 min with $s = 5.0$. Pat wants to know if humidity affects exercise behavior.

2. In an attempt to regulate the profession, the US Department of Health and Human Services has developed a fitness test for personal trainers. The test requires that the trainers must perform a series of exercises within a certain period of time. Normative data, collected in a nationwide test, reveal a normal distribution with an average completion time of $\mu = 92$ min and of $\sigma = 11$. Pat and four other Hollywood personal trainers (so $n = 5$) take the test. For these trainers, the average time to complete the task is averages 115 min. Pat is worried that the Hollywood personal trainers (in this sample) differ significantly from the norm.

3. Now, conduct the hypothesis tests for the examples given. Complete the hypothesis test for the tests you choose for Questions 1 and 2 (*z* or *t* test), showing all steps.

10B: ONE-SAMPLE *t* TEST IN SPSS

Use SPSS to complete the one-sample *t* test, and answer the questions for each study example that follows.

1. Suppose that your psychology professor, Dr. I. D. Ego, gives a 20-point true–false quiz to 9 students and wants to know if they were different from groups in the past who have tended to have an average of 9.0. Their scores from the current group were 6, 7, 7, 8, 8, 8, 9, 9, 10. Did the current group perform differently from those in the past? Assume a critical value of $\alpha = 0.05$.

2. The personnel department for a major corporation in the Northeast reported that the average number of absences during the months of January and February last year was $\mu = 7.4$. In an attempt to reduce absences, the company offered free flu shots to all employees this year. For a sample of $n = 10$ people who took the flu shots, the number of absences this year were 6, 8, 10, 3, 4, 6, 5, 4, 5, 6. Do these data indicate a significant *reduction* in the number of absences? Use $\alpha = .05$.

① (by hand)

$\bar{x} = 8$

$s = 1.118$

$\mu = 9.0$

$\dfrac{8-9}{1.118/\sqrt{9}} = -2.439$

$df\ (8)\ @\ \alpha\ 0.05\ 2\text{-tailed} = -2.306$

$t > t\,crit$

$-2.439 > -2.306$

reject null

10C: ONE-SAMPLE *t* TESTS BY HAND

Use a one-sample *t* test (calculated by hand) to answer the following questions.

1. Suppose that your psychology professor, Dr. I. D. Ego, wants to evaluate people's driving ability after 24 hr of sleep deprivation. She develops a test of driving skill (scores ranging from 1 [*bad driving*] to 10 [*excellent driving*]) and administers it to 101 drivers who have been paid to stay awake for 24 hr. The scores from the group had a mean of 4.5 and a standard deviation of 1.6. Determine if the sleep-deprived group mean is significantly different from the known population mean of 5.8 for the driving test. Assume $\alpha = .05$.

   [handwritten annotations:]
   H_0: sleep dep is not sig diff
   H_A: sleep dep grp is sig diff
   $\bar{x} = 4.5, s = 1.6 \quad n = 101$
   $\mu = 5.8$
   $t = \dfrac{4.5 - 5.8}{1.6/\sqrt{101}} = -8.02$
   $df(n) = 1.98$

2. Several years ago, a school survey revealed that the average age at which students first tried an alcoholic beverage was $\alpha = 14$ years (with a normal distribution). To determine if anything has changed, a random sample of five students was asked questions about alcohol use. The age at which drinking first began was reported as 11, 13, 14, 12, 10. Use these data to determine if there has been a change in the age at which drinking began. Use $\alpha = .05$.

3. A random sample of $n = 36$ scores has $X = 48$. Use this sample ($\alpha = .05$) to determine if the sample is different from the population with $\alpha = 45$ for each of the following situations:

   a. Sample $SS = 60$. (*Hint: SS* = sum of squares)

   b. Sample $SS = 600$.

   c. How does the sample variability contribute to the outcome of the test?

4. A national company is attempting to determine if they need to hire more employees. One thing they are basing this decision on is the number of hours per week their current employees work. They collect a sample of average hours worked per week from 30 employees to compare with the national full-time work standard of 40 hr per week. The mean number of hours worked for their sample is 47.8 with $SS = 1020$. Using $\alpha = .05$, conduct a test to determine if this company's employees work more hours per week than the national standard.

5. Scores on the SAT test are normally distributed with a $\mu = 500$ and a $\alpha = 100$. Dr. Ed Standards, the local district school superintendent, develops a new program that he believes should increase SAT scores for students. He selects 25 local high school students to take the program and then take the SAT test. His sample has an average SAT score of 559. Conduct a hypothesis test to determine whether this program works. Show all of your steps and state all of your assumptions.

6. Suppose that the school board tells Dr. Standards that the new program is too expensive to pilot on 25 students and asks that he reduce his sample size to 9 students. Assume the same properties for the population of SAT scores. Suppose that his sample of 9 students also has a mean score of 559. How does this reduction in sample size affect Dr. Standards' hypothesis test?

10D: RELATED-SAMPLES *t* TESTS

1. A major university would like to improve its tarnished image following a large on-campus scandal. Its marketing department develops a short television commercial and tests it on a sample of $n = 7$ subjects. People's attitudes about the university are measured with a short questionnaire, both before and after viewing the commercial. The data are as follows:

Person	X_1 (before)	X_2 (after)
A	15	15
B	11	13
C	10	18
D	11	12
E	14	16
F	10	10
G	11	19
H	10	20
I	12	13
J	15	18

   a. Is this a within-subjects or a matched samples design? Explain your answer.

   b. Conduct a hypothesis test (showing all steps) to determine if the university should spend money to air the commercial (i.e., did the commercial *improve* the attitudes?) Assume an α level = 0.05.

2. For the sample difference scores that follow, determine if the sample differs from $\mu_D = 0$. Use α = .01.

   Difference scores (D): 4, 5, 4, 2, 4, 5, 3, 5, 4

3. A researcher was interested in environmental effects on handedness. He measured the handedness of twins raised apart, where a positive score indicates more right-handedness and a negative score indicates more left-handedness (a score of 0 means the subject is ambidextrous). He used matched pairs of identical twins as subjects to rule out any genetic contribution to handedness scores (identical twins are the same genetically). The scores for each pair of twins are listed in the table that follows. Use these data to determine if the twins differ in handedness score (indicating that environment plays a role in handedness). Use α = .05.

Pair	Handedness score	
	Twin A	Twin B
1	+10	+11
2	−8	+3
3	−11	+11
4	+15	+10
5	0	+8
6	−4	+7

4. Each of the following sets of sample statistics comes from a within-subjects design.

Set 1: $n = 10$, $\overline{D} = +4.0$, $s = 10$

Set 2: $n = 10$, $\overline{D} = +4.0$, $s = 2$

Find t values. Even without looking up the critical t, for which set is it more likely to reject the H_0 indicating that the $\mu_D = 0$? Why?

10E: RELATED-SAMPLES *t* TEST IN SPSS

1. A psychology instructor teaches statistics. She wants to know if her lectures are helping her students understand the material. She tells students to read the chapter in the textbook before coming to class. Then before lecturing, the professor gives her class ($n = 10$) a short quiz on the material. Then she lectured on the same topic and followed her lecture with another quiz on the same material. Was there an effect of her lecture? Assume $\alpha = 0.05$ level. The data are as follows:

Person	X_1 (before)	X_2 (after)
A	85	85
B	81	83
C	70	78
D	91	92
E	84	88
F	70	70
G	91	89
H	80	90
I	72	73
J	85	88

   a. Enter the data into SPSS. Test your H_0 using a paired-samples *t* test. Do you reject the H_0?

   b. Use the Compute function to make a new variable that is the difference between the after-lecture quiz and the before-lecture quiz. Now use SPSS to compute a one-sample *t* test on this new difference column (use 0 as your test value). How do the results of this test compare with your answer in Question a? Why do you think this occurred?

10F: INDEPENDENT-SAMPLES *t* TESTS

1. A psychologist is interested in studying the effects of fatigue on mental alertness. She decides to study this question using a between-subjects design. She randomly assigns individuals to two groups (Group 1 stays awake for 24 hr; Group 2 goes to sleep). After this period, each subject is tested to see how well they detect a light on a screen. The dependent variable is the subjects' number of mistakes, which reflects their mental alertness. The higher the number, the less alert they are. Here are the results from the two groups:

	Group 1 (awake)	Group 2 (sleep)
n	5	10
mean	35	24
SS	120	270

Using an independent samples *t* test, answer the question of whether fatigue adversely affects mental alertness ($\alpha = 0.05$). (Do this one by hand.)

2. A psychology instructor at a large university teaches statistics. There are 22 students in the class, and he has broken them into two groups. Each group has a different graduate assistant (GA) who is responsible for running separate breakout lecture and lab sections of the course. One GA has lots of experience teaching, while the other has more limited experience. The instructor wants to check for comparable learning across the two GAs, hoping to find no difference. The data that follows are the scores (out of 100) of the students on the first midterm. Is there a difference between the groups? Assume an $\alpha = 0.05$ level. The data are as follows (notice that one group has more students than the other):

Group 1 (less experienced GA)	Group 2 (more experienced GA)
60	70
65	85
69	72
58	83
57	81
59	69
52	65
72	75
70	79
65	71
	89
	80

10G: HYPOTHESIS TESTING—MULTIPLE TESTS

1. A between-subjects design was conducted to compare two groups. Data were as follows:

   $\overline{X_A} = 58$, $\overline{X}_B = 52$

   $n_A = 4$, $n_B = 4$

   $SS_A = 84$, $SS_B = 108$

   a. Calculate the variance for each sample, and then compute the pooled variance. You should find that the pooled variance is exactly halfway between the two sample variances. Why is this true for this particular study?

   b. Do these data indicate a significant difference between the groups? Use a two-tailed test with $\alpha = .05$.

2. For two samples, one sample has $n = 6$ and $SS = 500$, while the other sample has $n = 9$ and $SS = 670$. If the sample mean difference is 15 points, is this difference large enough to be significant for $\alpha = .05$ with a two-tailed test?

3. Two people are arguing about the size of different breeds of dogs. One believes that German shepherds are larger than huskies, while the other person believes the opposite is true. They conduct a study to see which one of them is correct. They sample the weights of 10 dogs of each breed. The data are as follows:

   German Shepherds: 55, 72, 61, 43, 59, 70, 67, 49, 55, 63

   Huskies: 48, 77, 46, 51, 60, 44, 53, 61, 52, 41

   a. Should a one-tailed or two-tailed test be conducted? Why?

   b. Conduct the appropriate test with $\alpha = .05$. Which breed is larger, or are they the same?

4. Different designs affect the following set of data. Both tests will be to find any difference between treatments with $\alpha = .05$. (These data can represent either 10 different participants or 5 participants tested in each condition.)

Treatment 1	Treatment 2
10	11
2	5
1	2
15	18
7	9

   a. Assume that the data are from an independent samples experiment using two separate samples, each with five subjects. Use SPSS to test whether the data indicate a significant difference between the two treatments (assume $\alpha = .05$). List each step of the hypothesis testing procedure.

   b. Now assume that the data are from a repeated-measures design using one sample of five subjects, each of whom have been tested twice. Use SPSS to test whether the data indicate a significant difference between the two treatments (again assume $\alpha = .05$). Remember that you'll have to change the way the data are entered in the data window.

   c. You should find that the repeated measures design and the independent samples design reaches a different conclusion. How do you explain the differences? (*Hint:* Think about how sampling error is estimated for the two tests.)

10H: MORE HYPOTHESIS TESTS WITH MULTIPLE TESTS

1. A marine biologist is comparing the size of great white sharks in the Pacific and Atlantic Oceans to determine which ocean has the larger sharks. He takes a sample of 20 sharks—10 sharks from each ocean—and measures their lengths. The measurements for the 20 sharks are listed in the following table:

Shark lengths (in feet)			
Pacific Ocean		**Atlantic Ocean**	
1	18.2	11	16.1
2	15.8	12	14.3
3	13.6	13	14.7
4	19.7	14	15.7
5	19.1	15	19.6
6	12.2	16	15.3
7	16.8	17	13.2
8	22.8	18	15.8
9	16.6	19	15.2
10	16.8	20	16.2

2. A behavioral psychologist wants to know if food acts as a good motivator for rats to learn a maze faster than normal. She places a food pellet at the end of a maze that the rat can smell while working through the maze. She puts eight rats through the maze and records how long it takes them to find the food at the end. She already knows that without the food, rats as a population take an average of 28.9 s to run the maze (with a normal distribution). Using the following timing data recorded, determine if the rats learn the maze faster with the food pellet than without it.

    Times in seconds ($n = 8$): 25.6, 29.0, 23.1, 25.5, 28.7, 26.5, 25.4, 23.9

3. Two groups of participants ($n = 10$ per group, total $N = 20$) were given a problem-solving task. One group was told they had 5 min to complete the task. The other group was not told they had a time limit but was also given 5 min to complete the task. For both groups, the number of puzzles solved in the 5-min period was measured. These data for the 20 participants are listed in the table that follows. Conduct a hypothesis test to determine if an announced time limit affects the number of puzzles solved. Based on the outcome of the test, what can you conclude about the effect of an announced time limit?

Number solved			
Time limit announced		**No time limit announced**	
S1	6	S11	7
S2	8	S12	6
S3	5	S13	9
S4	4	S14	4
S5	6	S15	8
S6	9	S16	10
S7	8	S17	7
S8	5	S18	8
S9	4	S19	7
S10	5	S20	9

4. Does caffeine reduce depression? Participants in this study were 10 people who regularly consume something containing caffeine each day. During the study, however, each participant was barred from consuming caffeine not provided by the experimenter. They came to the lab two subsequent mornings and were given a pill. The pill either contained caffeine or was a placebo (i.e., each participant received both pills but on different days). The order of the pill received was counterbalanced (i.e., half received the caffeine pill first and the other half received it last). They completed a depression scale at the end of each day. Based on the depression scores that follow (higher scores mean more depression), does caffeine appear to reduce depression?

Depression scores		
Person	**Caffeine**	**Placebo**
1	5	16
2	5	23
3	4	5
4	3	7
5	8	14
6	5	24
7	0	6
8	0	3
9	2	15
10	11	

5. Whether a winning team can be purchased is a debated topic in baseball. Many major league team owners spend a lot of money on talented players to put together a team that they hope will win. Using the data that follows on 20 teams, conduct a test to compare batting averages for samples of players from the 10 teams with the highest payroll and 10 teams with the lowest payrolls to see if this practice is justified.

Batting averages			
Highest payroll		Lowest payroll	
Team 1	.275	Team 11	.289
Team 2	.301	Team 12	.255
Team 3	.225	Team 13	.267
Team 4	.325	Team 14	.333
Team 5	.350	Team 15	.233
Team 6	.210	Team 16	.300
Team 7	.240	Team 17	.245
Team 8	.200	Team 18	.285
Team 9	.315	Team 19	.292
Team 10	.301	Team 20	.310

10I: *t* TESTS SUMMARY WORKSHEET

A number of studies tested how amount of sleep affects test performance. In Study 1, a single sample was asked to sleep for 8 hr, and then their test performance was compared with the population $\mu = 70\%$. For Study 2, a single sample of students was asked to sleep for 8 hr before their first exam in a course and to stay up all night the night before their second exam in the course. For Study 3, a sample of students were randomly assigned to one of two groups, where one group slept for 8 hr the night before the exam and the other group stayed awake the night before the exam. For the following table, fill in the parts for each *t* test.

Test	When do you use this test?	Hypotheses H_0 & H_1			How do you run this test in SPSS?	Using SPSS, how do you know when to reject or fail to reject the H_0?
One-sample *t* FORMULA: Which study is this?		Two-tailed	One-tailed			
			IV (independent variable) ↑ DV (dependent variable)	IV ↓ DV		
Paired-samples *t* FORMULA: Which study is this?		Two-tailed	One-tailed			
			IV ↑ DV	IV ↓ DV		
Independent-sample *t* FORMULA: Which study is this?		Two-tailed	One-tailed			
			IV ↑ DV	IV ↓ DV		

10J: CHOOSE THE CORRECT *t* TEST

For each study description that follows, choose the correct inferential statistic to test the hypothesis.

1. A single sample is recruited to study the effects of caffeine on work productivity. Each participant in the study completes a task where he or she has to stack boxes on shelves for 15 min with and without caffeine. The researcher's hypothesis is that the participants will stack more boxes after drinking caffeine than without the caffeine.

    a. One-tailed one-sample *t* test

    b. Two-tailed one-sample *t* test

    c. One-tailed paired-samples *t* test

    d. Two-tailed paired-samples *t* test

2. A researcher is interested in the connection between sleep and depression. A group of students is recruited for the study based on their scores on a depression questionnaire. Students with a score in the top 75th percentile of the population of scores on the scale are placed in the "depressed" group, and students with a score in the bottom 25th percentile of the population of scores on the scale are placed in the "nondepressed" group. The researcher then asks the students to report the amount of sleep they have gotten on the past seven nights to compare the average number of sleep minutes per night across the two groups.

    a. One-tailed one-sample *t* test

    b. Two-tailed one-sample *t* test

    c. One-tailed paired-samples *t* test

    d. Two-tailed paired-samples *t* test

3. The score on a standardized test in the population is known to be $\mu = 500$. A sample of students completes a new curriculum designed to increase their skills that the test measures. The mean and standard deviation of the students' scores on the test is calculated after the new curriculum has been administered.

    a. One-tailed one-sample *t* test

    b. Two-tailed one-sample *t* test

    c. One-tailed paired-samples *t* test

    d. Two-tailed paired-samples *t* test

4. A developmental psychologist believes that working memory skills (i.e., the ability to keep track of multiple tasks at once) significantly increases between the ages of 5 and 8. She recruits children of these ages and gives them a working memory task to compare their scores age the groups.

    a. One-tailed one-sample *t* test

    b. Two-tailed one-sample *t* test

    c. One-tailed paired-samples *t* test

    d. Two-tailed paired-samples *t* test

5. You think that quizzing yourself before a final exam will help you do better on the test than just rereading your lecture notes, but you are concerned that using yourself as a test case will bias the results, so you recruit 10 of your friends who are willing to participate in your study to test your idea. Five of your friends say they reread their notes before tests, and five of them say they quiz themselves before tests. You compare the final exam scores of your friends in each group to test your hypothesis.

    a. One-tailed one-sample *t* test

    b. Two-tailed one-sample *t* test

    c. One-tailed paired-samples *t* test

    d. Two-tailed paired-samples *t* test

10K: WRITING A RESULTS SECTION FROM SPSS OUTPUT—*t* TESTS

A study was conducted where 36 participants completed an experiment where ads were presented subliminally during a task (e.g., Coke ads were flashed at very fast rates during movie ads). Participants were then given a recognition test for images in the ads: Two images were presented, and participants had to choose which one of the two was presented earlier. However, the researcher wanted to know if standard ads (e.g., a glass of Coke being poured over ice) were remembered differently than emotional ads (e.g., a person drinking a Coke is tightly hugging another person). To test this, each of the 36 participants completed the recognition task for both types of ads (i.e., when first presented, both types of ads were shown in a random order and recognition trials were included for both types of ads). Thus, each participant had a separate recognition score for standard and emotional ads.

The SPSS output for this study appears in the figure that follows. Use the output to write an American Psychological Association (APA)-style results section for this study.

t Test

Paired Samples Statistics

		Mean	N	Std. Deviation	Std. Error Mean
Pair 1	Standard Ads	53.5000	10	10.40566	3.29056
	Emotional Ads	66.3000	10	12.68464	4.01123

Paired Samples Correlations

		N	Correlation	Sig.
Pair 1	Standard Ads and Emotional Ads	10	.118	.745

Paired Samples Test

		Paired Differences							
					95% Confidence Interval of the Difference				
		Mean	Std. Deviation	Std. Error Mean	Lower	Upper	t	df	Sig. (2-tailed)
Pair 1	Standard Ads and Emotional Ads	−12.800	15.42581	4.87807	−23.835	−1.7650	−2.624	9	.028

11

ONE-WAY ANALYSIS OF VARIANCE

11A: ONE-WAY BETWEEN-SUBJECTS ANALYSIS OF VARIANCE (HAND CALCULATIONS)

A psychologist at a private mental hospital was asked to determine whether there was a clear difference in the length of stay for patients with different categories of diagnosis. Looking at the last four patients in each of the three major categories, the results (in terms of weeks of stay) were as follows.

Diagnosis category		
Affective disorders	Cognitive disorders	Drug-related conditions
7	12	8
6	8	10
5	9	12
6	11	10

Using an $\alpha = 0.05$ level, is there a significant difference in length of stay among diagnosis categories? Show all five steps of hypothesis testing.

11B: ONE-WAY BETWEEN-SUBJECTS ANALYSIS OF VARIANCE IN SPSS

1. Analyze the following data using SPSS:

Diagnosis category		
Affective disorders	Cognitive disorders	Drug-related conditions
7	12	8
6	8	10
5	9	12
6	11	10

   a. Using SPSS (and an $\alpha = 0.05$ level), is there a significant difference in length of stay among diagnosis categories? Compute the means and standard deviations for each group.

   b. Using Scheffe's test, test which groups are different from each other.

2. Using the Datafile_3.sav data file at **http://edge.sagepub.com/mcbridermstats1e**, test whether there are differences in university grade point average (GPA) for different majors. Compute the means and standard deviations for each group. Conduct planned comparisons to test whether computer majors are different from engineering majors and computer majors from other sciences.

11C: WRITING A RESULTS SECTION FROM SPSS OUTPUT—ANALYSIS OF VARIANCE

A study was conducted to examine the effect of text format on student satisfaction for two subject topics: Chemistry and Psychology. Text format was manipulated across student groups with paper, standard electronic, and interactive electronic text. Students taking either Introductory Chemistry or Introductory Psychology courses were recruited as participants in the study. Their satisfaction with their assigned text was measured at the end of the course on a 1 to 10 scale.

The SPSS output for this study appears in the following figures. Use the output to write an American Psychological Association (APA)-style results section for this study.

➡ ## Univariate Analysis of Variance

Between-Subjects Factors

		Value Label	N
Type of Text	1.00	Paper	40
	2.00	Standard Electronic	40
	3.00	Interactive Electronic	40
Subject Topic	1.00	Psychology	62
	2.00	Chemistry	58

Descriptive Statistics

Dependent Variable: Student Satisfaction Rating

Type of Text	Subject Topic	Mean	Std. Deviation	N
Paper	Psychology	4.8500	1.63111	20
	Chemistry	5.0000	1.55597	20
	Total	4.9250	1.57525	40
Standard Electronic	Psychology	5.2500	1.64845	24
	Chemistry	5.1875	2.00728	16
	Total	5.2250	1.77573	40
Interactive Electronic	Psychology	7.8333	1.94785	18
	Chemistry	7.4545	1.71067	22
	Total	7.6250	1.80721	40
Total	Psychology	5.8710	2.13083	62
	Chemistry	5.9828	2.07315	58
	Total	5.9250	2.09506	120

Tests of Between–Subjects Effects

Dependent Variable: Student Satisfaction Rating

Source	Type III Sum of Squares	df	Mean Square	F	Sig.	Partial Eta Squared
Corrected Model	176.883[a]	5	35.377	11.675	.000	.339
Intercept	4147.129	1	4147.129	1368.602	.000	.923
text	176.154	2	88.077	29.066	.000	.338
topic	.278	1	.278	.092	.763	.001
text * topic	1.408	2	.704	.232	.793	.004
Error	345.442	114	3.030			
Total	4735.000	120				
Corrected Total	522.325	119				

a. R Squared = .339 (Adjusted R Squared = .310)

Estimated Marginal Means

1. Type of Text

Estimates

Dependent Variable: Student Satisfaction Rating

Type of Text	Mean	Std. Error	95% Confidence Interval	
			Lower Bound	Upper Bound
Paper	4.925	.275	4.380	5.470
Standard Electronic	5.219	.281	4.662	5.775
Interactive Electronic	7.644	.277	7.096	8.192

Pairwise Comparisons

Dependent Variable: Student Satisfaction Rating

(I) Type of Text	(J) Type of Text	Mean Difference (I–J)	Std. Error	Sig.[b]	95% Confidence Interval for Difference[b]	
					Lower Bound	Upper Bound
Paper	Standard Electronic	–.294	.393	1.000	–1.249	.662
	Interactive Electronic	–2.719[*]	.390	.000	–3.667	–1.771
Standard Electronic	Paper	.294	.393	1.000	–.662	1.249
	Interactive Electronic	–2.425[*]	.394	.000	–3.383	–1.467
Interactive Electronic	Paper	2.719[*]	.390	.000	1.771	3.667
	Standard Electronic	2.425[*]	.394	.000	1.467	3.383

Based on estimated marginal means

*. The mean difference is significant at the

b. Adjustment for multiple comparisons: Bonferroni.

11D: INFERENTIAL STATISTICS AND ANALYSES

Listed in the table are 10 statements that are common pieces of cliché advice (many of which you may have heard at some point in your life). Pick two of the clichés, and design a study to test each one following the example here.

Absence makes the heart grow fonder.	Experience is the best teacher.
All work and no play make Jack a very dull boy.	An apple never falls far from the tree.
Good fences make good neighbors.	He who laughs last laughs longest.
Ignorance is bliss.	A rose by any other name still smells as sweet.
Opposites attract (relationships).	An apple a day keeps the doctor away.

Example: Laughter is the best medicine.

Null Hypothesis: Within the population, laughter is not the best medicine (is worse or as good as without it).

Alternative Hypothesis: Within the population, laughter is the best medicine.

Independent Variable: Laughter (presence vs. absence)

Dependent Variable: Physiological and Psychological Health (measured as difference scores between start and end of study)

Details: Between subjects or within subjects?

Why? Laughter should be done (between subjects) to avoid order effects.

Analysis Plan

One Sample *t* test Paired samples *t* test Independent Samples *t* test One-way analysis of variance (ANOVA)	Why? This is a within-subjects design with one independent variable that has two levels.

Cliché #1: Ignorance Is Bliss

_____

_____

Null Hypothesis: within the population, ignorance is not bliss

Alternative Hypothesis: win the population, ignorance is bliss

Independent Variable(s): ignorance (vs. not ignorance / knowledge)

Dependent Variable(s): bliss

Details: Between subjects or within subjects? Between

Why? because one subject cannot have the 2 levels of the independent variable: can't be ignorant and knowledgable without confunds of order effects.

_____

_____

_____

_____

Analysis Plan

	Why? _____
One sample *t* test	_____
Paired samples *t* test	_____
Independent samples *t* test	_____
One-Way ANOVA	_____

Cliché #2: An apple a day keeps the doctor away

_____

Null Hypothesis: w/in the population, a doctor is not kept away by an apple a day

Alternative Hypothesis: w/in the population, a doctor is kept away by an apple a day

Independent Variable(s): an apple (either per day or not per day)

Dependent Variable(s): doctor's presence (or absence), tested by having to go to the doctor

Details: Between subjects or within subjects? Between

Why? one person can't both have an apple everyday AND not have an apple everyday (ie: each treatment level can only be applied by itself to a participant) so it has to be between.

_____

Analysis Plan

	Why? _____
One sample *t* test	_____
Paired samples *t* test	_____
Independent samples *t* test	_____
One-way ANOVA	_____

12

CORRELATION TESTS AND SIMPLE LINEAR REGRESSION

12A: CREATING AND INTERPRETING SCATTERPLOTS

1. Josie conducted an honors research project in which she measured IQ scores and number of hours spent watching TV per week for several ISU students. Her results are shown in the graph. Each pair of numbers represents one student. The IQ score is shown first, and the number of hours of TV watched per week is shown next (for both variables, a higher score means more).

   a. On the graph shown, plot the data points for each student. Label each axis of the graph to indicate the variable plotted.

   b. Below the graph, identify the relationship as either positive, negative, or no correlation.

   c. Estimate the numerical correlation value (*r*) as a number between −1.0 to +1.0. Write your *r* estimate below the graph.

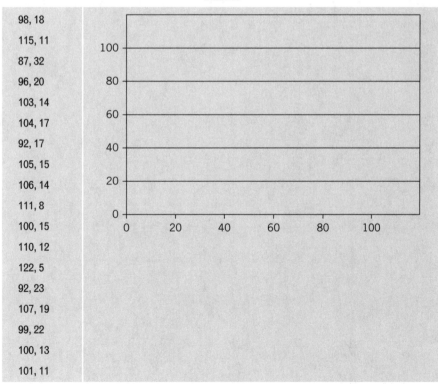

Scores

98, 18
115, 11
87, 32
96, 20
103, 14
104, 17
92, 17
105, 15
106, 14
111, 8
100, 15
110, 12
122, 5
92, 23
107, 19
99, 22
100, 13
101, 11

2. Each pair of variables below has a known relationship. Use common sense to determine what type of relationship likely exists between the variables.

   a. The number of times per day you smile at other people and the number of times per day others smile at you

   b. The number of hours per day a person studies and the number of exams per semester a person fails

   c. The number of gallons of water a person drinks in a week and the number of close friends the person has

   d. The number of alcoholic drinks a person has each week and their grade point average (GPA)

12B: UNDERSTANDING CORRELATIONS

1. Match the following graphs to the descriptions:

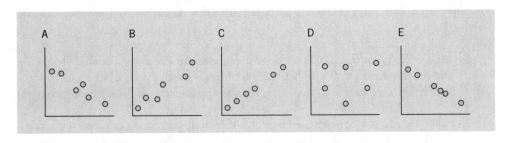

_____ Strong negative association

_____ Strong positive association

_____ Medium-strength negative association

_____ Medium-strength positive association

_____ No association

Computing Pearson's r (Sum of Squares [SS] Formula)

2. Make a table that looks like the one shown here, and complete the missing blanks (feel free to use a calculator).

	X	Y					
	0	1					
	10	3					
	4	1					
	8	2					
	8	3					
Sums	30	10					
Means	6	2					

Calculate sum of products (SP), SSx, SSy, & Pearson correlation (r).

12C: CORRELATIONS AND SCATTERPLOTS IN SPSS

Open the data set using the Datafile_4.sav data file at **http://edge.sagepub.com/mcbrider mstats1e.** This fictional data set contains the height, weight, age, and gender information for 40 individuals. Additionally, it has the average calcium intake, household income, and average parental height.

1. Make scatterplots that plot the relationship between the response variable "height" and the three quantitative explanatory variables (avgphgt, calcium, income). For each scatterplot, describe the nature of the relationship (in terms of direction and strength).

2. Make a scatterplot of height and weight, and include gender as a categorical variable (mark the cases by gender). How does the relationship between height and weight compare for men and women?

3. Compute a correlation matrix that computes the correlation coefficients between five of our variables (height, weight, income, calcium, avgphgt). Which variables have the strongest correlations? Which variables are negatively correlated?

12D: COMPUTING CORRELATIONS BY HAND

You conduct a survey on how much your friends like a website and whether it is related to their GPA. Your survey's response scale runs from 0 = *not like at all* to 5 = *absolutely love*. Your assignment is to provide all descriptive statistics for the following data set.

Person	Web liking	GPA	Person	Web liking	GPA
A	5	2.4	F	2	2.1
B	1	3.9	G	4	3.9
C	2	3.5	H	3	2.9
D	4	2.8	I	0	3.6
E	3	3.0	J	3	2.7

1. Make a scatterplot of both of your variables by entering the letter of each person on the proper place on the graph. Draw the best-fitting line through the set of points.

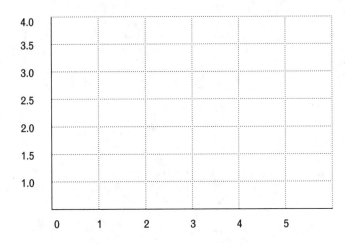

2. a. Find the following statistics for Xs and Ys for the preceding data. Show formulas and calculations.

   X Y

   Mode =

   Median =

   Range =

   Mean *(M)* =

   SS =

   Variance =

   Standard deviation (*SD*) =

   b. Find the following statistic for Xs and Ys together. Show formulas and calculations.

   Pearson *r* =

12E: HYPOTHESIS TESTING WITH CORRELATION USING SPSS

1. To measure the relationship between anxiety and test performance, a researcher asked his students to come to the lab 15 min before they were to take an exam in his class. The researcher measured the students' heart rates and then matched these scores with their exam performance after they had taken the exam. Use the following data and SPSS to conduct a hypothesis test for the correlation between anxiety and test performance in the population. Use $\alpha = .05$.

Student	Heart rate	Exam score
A	76	78
B	81	68
C	60	88
D	65	80
E	80	90
F	66	68
G	82	60
H	71	95
I	66	84
J	75	75
K	80	62
L	76	51
M	77	63
N	79	71

12F: REGRESSION

1. A set of X and Y scores have a mean of X of 4, SS of 15, mean of Y of 5, and SP of 30.
   a. What is the regression equation for predicting Y from X?
   b. What are the predicted Y scores for the following X scores: 3, -2, 5, 6

2. Find the regression equation for predicting Y from X for the following set of scores. (Show your work for each step.)

   $X\ Y$

   0 9

   1 7

   2 11

3. Find the regression equation and standard error of estimate for the following set of data. (Show your work for each step.)

   $X\ Y$

   4 1

   7 16

   3 4

   5 7

   6 7

4. When a correlation is close to + 1.0, then the standard error of the estimate will be _____. When the correlation is close to 0, then the standard error of estimate will be _____.
   a. large, small
   b. close to 1.0, close to 0
   c. small, large
   d. cannot tell from the information given

13

CHI-SQUARE TESTS

13A: CHI-SQUARE CROSSTABS TABLES

1. Suppose that you're interested in whether there is a relationship between gender and membership in an after-school club (in high school students). So, you randomly selected 30 students from a local high school and recorded their gender and whether or not they were members of an after-school club. Create a cross tabulation for the following data.

Person number	Gender	Club membership
1	Male	Non-club member
2	Female	Club member
3	Male	Non-club member
4	Male	Club member
5	Female	Non-club member
6	Female	Non-club member
7	Male	Club member
8	Male	Non-club member
9	Male	Non-club member
10	Female	Club member
11	Female	Non-club member
12	Female	Non-club member
13	Female	Club member
14	Female	Club member
15	Female	Club member
16	Female	Non-club member
17	Male	Non-club member
18	Male	Club member
19	Female	Non-club member
20	Male	Non-club member

Person number	Gender	Club membership
21	Female	Non-club member
22	Male	Non-club member
23	Male	Non-club member
24	Male	Club member
25	Male	Club member
26	Female	Club member
27	Female	Non-club member
28	Male	Non-club member
29	Female	Non-club member
30	Female	Non-club member

2. For the following voting survey data, create a crosstabs table and then conduct a test to determine if the two variables are related. Use $\alpha = .01$.

Person	Gender	Plans to vote for	Person	Gender	Plans to vote for
1	Male	Trump	16	Female	Clinton
2	Male	Trump	17	Male	Trump
3	Female	Trump	18	Male	Clinton
4	Female	Clinton	19	Female	Trump
5	Female	Clinton	20	Female	Trump
6	Male	Clinton	21	Male	Clinton
7	Male	Trump	22	Female	Clinton
8	Female	Clinton	23	Male	Trump
9	Female	Trump	24	Female	Clinton
10	Male	Clinton	25	Female	Trump
11	Male	Trump	26	Male	Trump
12	Female	Trump	27	Female	Clinton
13	Male	Clinton	28	Male	Trump
14	Female	Clinton	29	Female	Clinton
15	Male	Trump	30	Male	Trump

13B: CHI-SQUARE HAND CALCULATIONS FROM CROSSTABS TABLES

1. Gender differences in dream content are well documented. Suppose that a researcher studies aggression content in the dreams of men and women. Each subject reports his or her most recent dream. Then each dream is judged by a panel of experts to have low, medium, or high aggression content. The observed frequencies are shown in the following table. Is there a relationship between gender and the aggression content of dreams? Test with $\alpha = 0.01$. Be sure to state your hypotheses.

		Aggression content		
		Low	Medium	High
Gender	Female	18	4	2
	Male	4	17	15

2. New research seems to suggest that kids raised in homes with pets tend to have fewer allergies than kids raised without pets. A survey study was conducted to test this finding. A sample of 100 adults were asked if they had allergies (no or yes) and how many pets they had between the ages of 1 and 10 years old (0, 1, 2 or more). Use the following crosstabs table to conduct a chi-square test with $\alpha = .05$. Indicate whether these data support the previous findings or not.

# Pets/ Allergies	0	1	2 or more
No	10	25	35
Yes	15	10	5

13C: CHI-SQUARE IN SPSS—TYPE IN THE DATA

Using SPSS, compute the marginals and expected values and chi-square for the data in the following table.

Suppose that you're interested in whether there is a relationship between gender and membership in an after-school club (in high school students). So, you randomly selected 30 students from a local high school and recorded their gender and whether or not they were members of an after-school club. Create a cross tabulation for the following data.

Person number	Gender	Club membership
1	Male	Non-club member
2	Female	Club member
3	Male	Non-club member
4	Male	Club member
5	Female	Non-club member
6	Female	Non-club member
7	Male	Club member
8	Male	Non-club member
9	Male	Non-club member
10	Female	Club member
11	Female	Non-club member
12	Female	Non-club member
13	Female	Club member
14	Female	Club member
15	Female	Club member
16	Female	Non-club member
17	Male	Non-club member
18	Male	Club member
19	Female	Non-club member
20	Male	Non-club member
21	Female	Non-club member
22	Male	Non-club member
23	Male	Non-club member
24	Male	Club member
25	Male	Club member
26	Female	Club member
27	Female	Non-club member
28	Male	Non-club member
29	Female	Non-club member
30	Female	Non-club member

13D: CHI-SQUARE IN SPSS FROM A DATA FILE

For the following questions, download the file Datafile_1.sav at http://edge.sagepub.com/mcbridermstats1e.

1. Were juniors and seniors more likely than freshmen and sophomores to attend the review sessions? Provide a bar chart showing the breakdown. Assuming $\alpha = 0.05$, test whether these variables are independent. Remember to state your hypotheses.

2. Were men more likely than women to do an extra credit assignment? Report the number of people who did and didn't do the extra credit project broken down by gender. Assuming an $\alpha = 0.05$, test whether gender and extra credit participation are independent. Remember to state your hypotheses.

14

MULTIFACTOR EXPERIMENTS AND TWO-WAY ANALYSIS OF VARIANCE (CHAPTERS 14 AND 15)

14A: FACTORIAL DESIGNS

1. Consider the following data from a factorial-design experiment. The dependent variable was "percentage of participants who offered help to a stranger in distress."

Number of bystanders	Gender of stranger	
	Male	Female
0	30	90
10	10	50

a. What is the design of this study (e.g., 2 × 2, 2 × 3)?

b. List the independent variables of this study, and list the levels of each.

c. Sketch a graph of the results of the study. Fill in the names and levels of the independent variables.

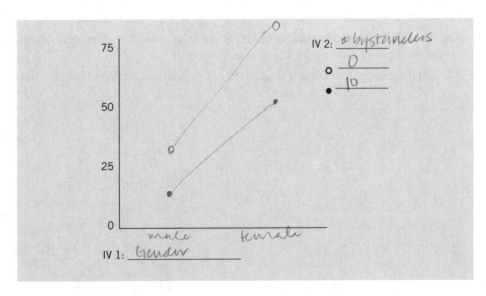

d. *Main Effects:* On the average, how does the number of bystanders affect helping? On the average, how does the gender of the stranger in need affect helping?

e. Do the graphed data suggest the presence of an interaction effect? If so, describe it.

2. In the following summarized factorial design experiment, the dependent variable was "average number of hallucinations."

Dose of drug	Type of drug	
	LSD	**Marijuana**
Low	3	1
Medium	5	2
High	13	3

a. What is the design of this study (e.g., 2 × 2, 2 × 3)?

b. Sketch a graph of the results of the study. Fill in the names.

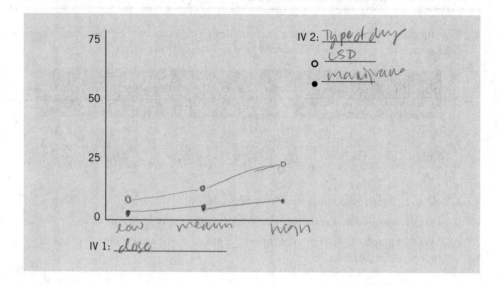

c. *Main Effects:* For each factor and levels of the independent variables, state whether a main effect appears to exist. If one does, describe it.

d. Do the graphed data suggest the presence of an interaction effect? If so, describe it.

14B: FACTORIAL DESIGNS ARTICLE—SPROESSER, SCHUPP, AND RENNER (2014)

For this exercise, download the following article (it can be found on the SAGE Student Site):

Sproesser, G., Schupp, H. T., & Renner, B. (2014). The bright side of stress-induced eating: Eating more when stressed but less when pleased. *Psychological Science, 25,* 58–65.

The researchers in this study were interested in how social situations can influence stress-induced eating. They grouped subjects according to self-reported stress-induced eating habits: consistently eating more (hyperphagics) or eating less (hypophagics) when stressed. Each subject was then exposed to one of three social situations: (1) a social inclusion condition, where subjects were told that a confederate partner had approved of a video they had made answering some questions and was looking forward to meeting them, (2) a neutral condition, where they were told their partners could not meet them because their partners had to cancel their participation, or (3) a social exclusion condition, where they were told that their partner had decided not to meet them after viewing their video. Subjects were then given an ice cream taste test, and the amount of ice cream consumed was measured.

Use this description to help you answer the following questions:

1. What is the independent variable in this study, and what are its levels?

2. The researchers also included a subject or attribute variable in this study. What was this subject variable? How were subjects classified on this variable?

The results of the experiment are displayed in the following graph:

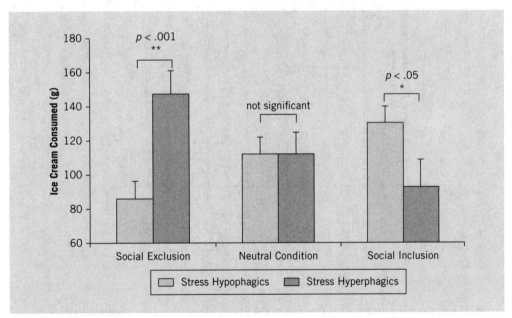

Source: Sproesser et al., 2014.

3. Does this graph indicate a main effect of social condition? Explain your answer.

4. Does this graph indicate a main effect of eating phagic group? Explain your answer.

5. Does this graph indicate the presence of an interaction? If so, describe the interaction.

14C: FACTORIAL DESIGNS ARTICLE—
FARMER, MCKAY, AND TSAKIRIS (2014)

For this exercise, download the following article (it can be found on the SAGE Student Site):

Farmer, H., McKay, R., & Tsakiris, M. (2014). Trust in me: Trustworthy others are seen as more physically similar to the self. *Psychological Science, 25,* 290–292.

1. Describe the study. Make sure to include the following information:
   - What is/are the dependent variable(s)?
   - What is/are the independent variable(s)?
   - For each independent variable, how many levels does it have?
   - For each independent variable, is it manipulated between or within groups?
   - How many total conditions are there in the study?

2. What are the hypotheses for each independent variable (main effect predictions)?

3. What is the hypothesis for the interaction?

The results presented in the following graph show the mean percentage of the trustee's face that was present in the photos judged to be at the point of subjective equality (PSE) as a function of the conditions of the experiment.

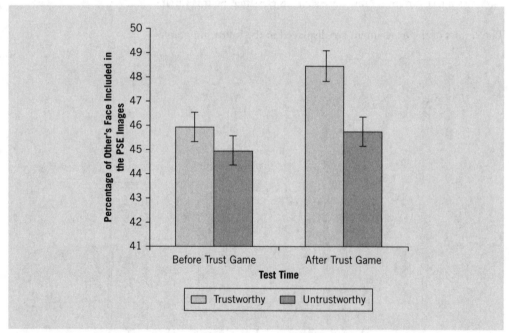

Source: McKay and Tsakiris, 2014.

4. Describe the pattern of results seen in the graph. Does the pattern suggest that an interaction is present? If so, describe the interaction; if not, describe why the pattern does not indicate an interaction.

5. What do the statistical outcomes in the results section tell you about the main effects and interaction? (*Note:* This question should only be answered if downloading the article and reading the results section was assigned.)

6. What do these results tell us about the hypotheses for this study?

14D: DESCRIBING MAIN EFFECTS AND INTERACTIONS

The following data sets are from a factorial design study examining the effects of group and individual therapy over two different lengths of time. For each data set, determine what effects (both main effects and the interaction) are significant. For simplicity, assume that the data are ideal, meaning that any difference between means is a significant difference—no sampling error. Make a bar graph of each significant effect, and provide a verbal description of the effect.

a.

Length	Therapy type	
	Group	Individual
1 week	100	100
6 weeks	500	500

b.

Length	Therapy type	
	Group	Individual
1 week	300	700
6 weeks	200	400

c.

Length	Therapy type	
	Group	Individual
1 week	100	400
6 weeks	400	100

d.

Length	Therapy type	
	Group	Individual
1 week	250	100
6 weeks	250	400

14E: FACTORIAL ANALYSIS OF VARIANCE

Carry out an analysis of variance (ANOVA) for the following data set, including making a table of cell and marginal means and making a bar graph of the cell means. Use an alpha level of 0.05.

Participant	Level for IV_A	Level for IV_B	DV
A	1	1	9
B	1	1	7
C	1	2	3
D	1	2	1
E	2	1	1
F	2	1	3
G	2	2	7
H	2	2	9
I	3	1	1
J	3	1	3
K	3	2	7
L	3	2	9
M	4	1	9
N	4	1	7
O	4	2	3
P	4	2	1

Note: IV = independent variable; DV = dependent variable.

14F: ANALYSIS OF VARIANCE REVIEW

1. Patients with two kinds of diagnoses were randomly assigned to one of three types of therapy. The table of data is presented here. There were two patients per cell. Use SPSS to compute the results listed here. Use an alpha level of 0.05.

   a. Carry out the analysis of variance.

   b. Compute the cell and marginal means.

   c. Make a graph of the results.

   d. Describe the results in words.

   e. Compute the effect size of the statistics.

	Therapy		
	A	B	C
Diagnosis I	6	3	2
	2	1	4
Diagnosis II	11	7	8
	9	9	10

2. When participants memorize a list of words serially (in the order of presentation), words at the beginning and end of the list are remembered better than words in the middle. This has been called the serial-position effect. You wonder whether this holds true across different presentation modalities (reading lists versus hearing lists). You give a group of four people two lists of words: one they heard read to them and the other they read to themselves. Then you look at the number of words recalled from the first part of the list, the middle part of the list, and the final part of the list. The data are as follows:

Heard			Read		
Start of list	Middle of list	End of list	Start of list	Middle of list	End of list
1	5	0	1	3	0
3	7	2	4	4	1
5	6	1	6	6	3
3	2	1	2	5	0

   Is there a serial position effect for both methods? Are there main effects? Describe your results in a short paragraph that includes the relevant statistics, including descriptive statistics for conditions and levels of the independent variables. Assume an alpha level of 0.05.

3. For this problem, download and use the Datafile_3.sav data file **at http://edge.sagepub .com/mcbridermstats1e.**

   a. Test whether university grade point average (GPA) differs by gender and major. Describe the main effects and interactions (using means and a graph).

   b. Examine whether there is an interaction between type of SAT test performance (math or verbal) and gender. Describe your results in a short paragraph.

14G: MAIN EFFECTS AND INTERACTIONS IN FACTORIAL ANALYSIS OF VARIANCE

A sports psychologist studied the effect of a motivational program on number of injuries in one year among players of three different sports. The following chart shows the design. For each of the following possible patterns of results, make up a set of cell means, complete the table with the missing condition means according to the effect(s) listed, figure the marginal means, and make a bar graph of the results in the space at the right:

1. A main effect for type of sport and no other main effect or interaction

	Sport		
	Baseball	Football	Basketball
With motivational program	5	7	9
Without motivational program			

2. A main effect for program and no other main effect or interaction

	Sport		
	Baseball	Football	Basketball
With motivational program	5	5	5
Without motivational program			

3. Both main effects but no interaction

	Sport		
	Baseball	Football	Basketball
With motivational program	5	7	9
Without motivational program			

4. No main effect for program or sport but an interaction

	Sport		
	Baseball	Football	Basketball
With motivational program	5	7	9
Without motivational program			

15

ONE-WAY WITHIN-SUBJECTS ANALYSIS OF VARIANCE

15A: ONE-WAY WITHIN-SUBJECTS ANALYSIS OF VARIANCE

The following data were obtained from a research study examining the effect of sleep deprivation on motor skills performance. A sample of five participants was tested on a motor-skills task after 24 hr of sleep deprivation, tested again after 36 hr, and tested once more after 48 hr. The dependent variable is the number of errors made on the motor-skills task.

Participant	24 hr	36 hr	48 hr
A	0	1	5
B	0	0	0
C	1	3	5
D	0	1	5
E	4	5	9

Using an alpha level of 0.05, test whether or not these data indicate that the number of hours of sleep deprivation has a significant effect on motor-skills performance. List all of your steps of hypothesis testing.

15B: ONE-WAY WITHIN-SUBJECTS ANALYSIS OF VARIANCE IN SPSS

1. Use SPSS to analyze the following data.

Participant	24 hr	36 hr	48 hr
A	0	1	5
B	0	0	0
C	1	3	5
D	0	1	5
E	4	5	9

What can you conclude from your analysis?

15C: ONE-WAY WITHIN-SUBJECTS ANALYSIS OF VARIANCE REVIEW

1. It has been suggested that pupil size increases during emotional arousal. A researcher would, therefore, like to see whether the increase in pupil size is a function of the type of arousal (pleasant versus aversive). A random sample of five participants is selected for the study. Each participant views all three stimuli: (1) neutral, (2) pleasant, and (3) aversive photographs. The neutral photograph portrays a plain brick building. The pleasant photograph consists of a young man and woman sharing a large ice cream cone. Finally, the aversive stimulus is a graphic photograph of an automobile accident. Upon viewing each stimulus, the pupil size is measured (in millimeters) with sophisticated equipment. The data are as follows. Test whether all groups are equal (assume an alpha level of 0.05):

Participant	Stimulus		
	Neutral	Pleasant	Aversive
A	4	8	3
B	3	6	3
C	2	5	2
D	3	3	6
E	3	8	1

2. Use the same data given in Question 1, but treat it as though the experimenters used a between-groups design (different groups for each stimulus type). How do the results differ from what you obtained in Question 1? Explain why this is. Which design leads to a statistically more powerful test?

Stimulus		
Neutral	Pleasant	Aversive
4	8	3
3	6	3
2	5	2
3	3	6
3	8	1

3. A human factors psychologist studied three computer keyboard designs. Three samples of individuals were given material to type on a particular keyboard, and the number of errors committed by each participant was recorded. Are the groups the same? Use both an analysis of variance (ANOVA) and Tukey post hoc tests to answer this question. The data are as follows:

Keyboard A	Keyboard B	Keyboard C
0	6	6
4	8	5
0	5	9
1	4	4
0	2	6

16

MEET THE FORMULAE AND PRACTICE COMPUTATION PROBLEMS

16A: MEET THE FORMULA AND PRACTICE PROBLEMS: *z* SCORE TRANSFORMATION

Transforming a raw score into a *z* score is useful for locating a score in a distribution and is especially useful for comparing scores from different distributions.

Here is the formula:

$$z \text{ score} = \frac{X - \mu}{\sigma}$$

Using this formula, follow the steps:

Step 1: Compute the deviation score (score minus the mean).

Step 2: Divide by the standard deviation (*SD*).

The resulting transformed score has the following properties:

- The direction is indicated by the negative or positive sign on the deviation score.

- The distance from the mean is the value of the deviation score.

Suppose that you are a 5 ft 7 in tall male who weighs 180 lb. You want to know if you weigh more than you "should" given that you consider yourself somewhat short. Comparing your weight and height can be difficult because the two are measured on different scales. You can use *z* scores to directly compare the two scores. Suppose that for men over the age of 20 in the United States, their mean height is 69 in (*SD* = 3) and their mean weight is 190 lb (*SD* = 36).

Step 1

1. Compute the deviation score for height. Do the same for weight.

2. For each, is your deviation score above or below the mean? Can you easily tell if you are "too heavy" for your weight? Why or why not?

Step 2

1. Divide each of your deviation scores by their standard deviations.

2. Compare how much you differ from the averages for height and weight in terms of *z* scores. Is it easier to make a conclusion about whether you are "too heavy"? How does transforming the raw scores into standardized *z* scores help make the comparison?

16B: MEET THE FORMULA AND PRACTICE PROBLEMS: SINGLE-SAMPLE z TESTS AND t TESTS

Single-sample z tests and t tests are used when comparing single samples to the mean of a known population of samples. The two formulae are very similar to one another.

Here are the formulae:

Single-sample z test	Single-sample t test
$z = \dfrac{\bar{X} - \mu}{\sigma}$	$t = \dfrac{\bar{X} - \mu}{s_{\bar{X}}}$
$\sigma_{\bar{X}} = \dfrac{\sigma}{\sqrt{n}}$	$s_{\bar{X}} = \dfrac{s}{\sqrt{n}}$

Use the following formulae:

Step 1: Compute the deviation score (the sample mean minus the population mean).

Step 2: Compute either the standard error or the estimated standard error.

Step 3: Divide the deviation score by the standard error or the estimated standard error.

1. Compare the single-sample z test formula with the z score formula used to locate a single score in a distribution. How are the formulae similar, and how do they differ?

2. Compare the single-sample z test formula with the single-sample t test formula. How are these formulae similar and different?

3. Suppose that you took a standardized test with a mean of 500 and a standard deviation of 100.

   a. If you received a score of 630 on the test, what is the probability of getting that score or better?

   b. Suppose that you and a group of your three friends scored 670, 570, 690, and 590 on the test. What is the probability of getting the mean of these scores or better?

c. Suppose that you and a group of your three friends scored 670, 570, 690, and 590 on the test, but you don't know the population standard deviation. (*Hint:* This means you cannot calculate a z score for the mean.) Is the probability of getting the sample mean for these scores greater than .05 or not?

d. How do the three different scenarios (in a, b, and c) compare with each other? Examine the components of the formulae. How do the numerators compare? How do the denominators compare?

16C: MEET THE FORMULA AND PRACTICE PROBLEMS: COMPARING INDEPENDENT SAMPLES AND RELATED SAMPLES *t* TESTS

The formula that is used to compare two groups depends on the assumptions of the designs used to generate the data. If the two groups are composed of independent observations, then an independent samples *t* test is used. However, if the two groups of observations are related, then the related samples *t* test is used.

Here are the formulae:

Independent samples *t* test	Related samples *t* test
$t = \dfrac{\left(\bar{X}_A - \bar{X}_B\right) - \left(\mu_A - \mu_B\right)}{s_{\bar{X}_A - \bar{X}_B}}$	$t = \dfrac{\bar{D} - \mu_D}{s_{\bar{D}}}$
$s_{\bar{X}_A - \bar{X}_B} = \sqrt{\dfrac{s_p^2}{n_A} + \dfrac{s_p^2}{n_B}}$	$s_{\bar{D}} = \dfrac{s_D}{\sqrt{n_D}}$
$s_p^2 = \dfrac{SS_A + SS_B}{df_A + df_B}$	$s_D = \sqrt{\dfrac{SS_D}{n_D - 1}} = \sqrt{\dfrac{\left(D - \bar{D}\right)^2}{n_D - 1}}$

1. Compare the numerator portion of the two *t* tests.

    a. How are the $\left(\bar{X}_A - \bar{X}_B\right)$ and $\bar{D}$ parts of the formulae similar? How are they different?

    b. How are the $(\mu_A - \mu_B)$ and the μ_D parts of the formulae similar? How are they different?

2. Compare the denominator portion of the two tests.

    a. How are the two estimated standard errors ($s_{\bar{X}_A - \bar{X}_B}$ and $s_{\bar{D}}$) similar, and how are they different? Why does the independence of the two groups of observations lead to these differences?

    b. How are the variance formulae (s_p^2 and s_D) similar and different? Why does the independence of the two groups of observations lead to these differences?

3. Consider the following set of data.

Group A	Group B
45	43
55	49
40	35
60	51

a. Analyze the data, assuming that the two groups of observations are independent.

b. Analyze the data, assuming that the two groups of observations are related.

c. Explain why the conclusions that you draw in a and b are different, given that the numbers that you start with are identical.

16D: MEET THE FORMULA AND PRACTICE PROBLEMS: ONE-FACTOR BETWEEN-SUBJECTS ANALYSIS OF VARIANCE

Suppose that you want to see if there is an effect of an independent variable with three between-subjects levels. Consider the following data.

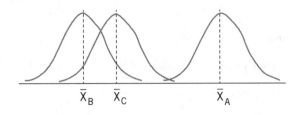

Total Variance

$$SS_{Total} = \Sigma(X - \bar{X}_{Total})^2$$

$$df_{Total} = N - 1$$

Between Groups Variance

$$SS_{Between} = n\Sigma(\bar{X}_{Group} - \bar{X}_{Total})^2$$

$$df_{Between} = a - 1$$

$$MS_{Between} = \frac{SS_{Between}}{df_{Between}}$$

Within Group Variance

$$SS_{Within} = \Sigma(SS_{Group})$$

$$df_{Within} = a(n - 1)$$

$$MS_{Within} = \frac{SS_{Within}}{df_{Within}}$$

Group A	Group B	Group C
10	5	4
7	1	6
5	3	9
10	7	3
8	4	3

ANOVA stands for analysis of variance. The goal of this procedure is to partition the total overall variance into two components, variance coming from within each group, and variance coming between each of the groups. Essentially, the process is like that used when computing variance and standard deviation. However, instead of doing that for one group, here variance is considered with several different groupings.

Use the following formulae:

Computing Total Variance (Variance for the Entire Set of Observations)

Step 1: Compute the grand mean ($\bar{X}_{Grand}$). Add up all the scores, and divide by the total number of scores.

Step 2: Compute the SS_{Total}. Find the deviation scores (subtract the grand mean from each score), square the deviation scores, and add all the deviation scores together.

Step 3: Compute the df_{Total}, the total number of scores – 1.

Step 4: Compute the MS_{Total} (total variance; MS = mean square).

- Compare this step with the steps used earlier for computing variance and standard deviation. What are the similarities and the differences?

Use the following formulae:

Computing Within Groups Variance (Variance for Groups A, B, and C Separately)

Step 1: Compute the mean of each group (A, B, and C).

Step 2: Compute the SS for each group. For each group, separately find the deviation scores, square the deviation scores, and add all the deviation scores together.

Step 3: Compute the df_{group} for each group, the total number of scores in the group – 1.

Step 4: Compute the SS_{Within}. Add up the SS from each group.

Step 5: Compute the df_{Within}. Add up the df from each group.

Step 6: Compute the MS_{Within}. Divide the SS_{Within} by the df_{Within}.

- Compare this step with the steps used earlier for computing variance and standard deviation. What are the similarities and the differences?

Use the following formulae:

Computing Between Groups Variance (Variance Across Groups A, B, and C)

Step 1: Compute the mean of each group (A, B, and C).

Step 2: Compute the SS for between groups (SS_{Between}). Find the deviation scores between the group means and the grand mean (GM), square the deviation scores, weight the deviation scores by the number of scores in the group, and add all the weighted deviation scores together.

Step 3: Compute the df_{Between}, the number of groups – 1.

Step 4: Compute the MS_{Between}. Divide the SS_{Between} by the df_{Between}.

- Compare this step with the steps used earlier for computing variance and standard deviation. What are the similarities and the differences?

Use the following formulae:

Computing the *F* ratio

Compare the variance between groups with the variance within groups. Divide the MS_{Between} by the MS_{Within}.

- How is the *F* ratio similar to the final ratio used in the independent samples *t* test?

16E: MEET THE FORMULA AND PRACTICE PROBLEMS: TWO-FACTOR ANALYSIS OF VARIANCE

Suppose that you want to see if there are effects of two separate independent variables tested in the same experimental design. The analysis that you can do is a two-factor ANOVA. In addition to testing the effect of each of the independent variables, the factorial ANOVA will also allow you to test whether the two variables also interact with each other. Consider the following data.

Factor A		Factor B		
		B_1	B_2	B_3
A_1	S_1	3	3	0
	S_2	0	8	0
	S_3	6	0	3
	S_4	2	3	0
A_2	S_1	0	3	0
	S_2	2	3	5
	S_3	3	5	8
	S_4	0	2	4

Since ANOVA stands for analysis of variance, the goal of this procedure is to partition the total overall variance into two components, variance coming from within each group, and variance coming between each of the groups. Essentially, the process is like that used when computing variance and standard deviation. However, instead of doing that for one group, here variance is considered with several different groupings. The first partition that is made is the same as that used for the one-factor between-subjects ANOVA analysis. However, because there is more than one independent variable, the variability is further partitioned in additional ways.

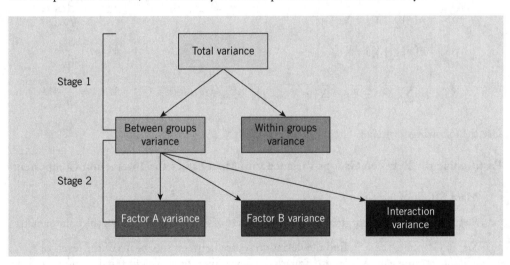

$$SS_{\text{Total}} = \sum \left(X - \overline{X}_{\text{Grand}} \right)^2 \qquad df_{\text{Total}} = N - 1 \qquad MS_{\text{Total}} = \frac{SS_{\text{Total}}}{df_{\text{Total}}}$$

Use the following formulae:

Computing Total Variance (Variance for the Entire Set of Observations)

Step 1: Compute the grand mean ($\overline{X}_{\text{Grand}}$). Add up all the scores, and divide by the total number of scores.

Step 2: Compute the SS_{Total}. Find the deviation scores (subtract the grand mean from each score), square the deviation scores, and add all the deviation scores together.

Step 3: Compute the df_{Total}, the total number of scores $- 1$.

Step 4: Compute the MS_{Total} (total variance).

- Compare this step with the steps used earlier for computing total variance in the one-factor ANOVA analysis.

$$SS_{Within} = \sum \left(X - \overline{X}_{AB} \right)^2 \qquad df_{Within} = (a)^*(b)(n-1) \qquad MS_{Within} = \frac{SS_{Within}}{df_{Within}}$$

Use the following formulae:

Computing Within-Groups Variance (Variance for Each of the Conditions, All Six Groups)

Step 1: Compute the mean of each group.

Step 2: Compute the SS for each group. For each group, separately find the deviation scores, square the deviation scores, and add all the deviation scores together.

Step 3: Compute the SS_{Within}, compute the SS for each condition separately, and then add up the SS from each group.

Step 4: Compute the df_{Within}. Multiply the # of levels of A by the # of levels of B by the number of participants in each condition.

Step 5: Compute the MS_{Within}. Divide the SS_{Within} by the df_{Within}.

- Compare this step with the steps used earlier for computing within variance in the one-factor ANOVA analysis.

$$SS_{A} = n(b)\sum \left(\overline{X}_A - \overline{X}_{Grand} \right)^2 \qquad df_A = a - 1 \qquad MS_A = \frac{SS_{Within}}{df_{Within}}$$

$$SS_{B} = n(a)\sum \left(\overline{X}_B - \overline{X}_{Grand} \right)^2 \qquad df_B = b - 1 \qquad MS_B = \frac{SS_{Within}}{df_{Within}}$$

$$SS_{AB} = n\sum \left(\overline{X}_{AB} - \overline{X}_{AB} - \overline{X}_B + \overline{X}_{Grand} \right)^2 \qquad df_{AB} = (a)*(b)(n-1) \qquad MS_{AB} = \frac{SS_{Within}}{df_{Within}}$$

Use the following formulae:

Partitioning the Between Groups Variance Into Main Effect and Interaction Components

Main Effect of A

Step 1: Compute the marginal mean of each level of each variable (across the columns).

Step 2: Compute the SS_A, find the deviation scores between the means of the levels of A and the grand mean (X – grand), square the deviation scores, weight the deviation scores by the number of scores in the group and the number of levels of B, and add all the weighted deviation scores together.

Step 3: Compute the df_A, the number of levels $- 1$.

Step 4: Compute the MS_A, divide the SS_A by the df_A.

For the main effect of B repeat the steps just given but for the B conditions instead of A (so use the marginal means down the columns).

Interaction

Step 1: Use marginal means for A and B (from the main effect steps).

Step 2: Compute the SS_{AB}. The deviation scores are more complex here. In each condition subtract the corresponding marginal mean of both A ($\overline{X}_A$) and B ($\overline{X}_B$) from the condition mean ($\overline{X}_{AB}$). Then add the grand mean ($\overline{X}_{Grand}$). Square the deviation scores, add all the weighted deviation scores together, and weight the deviation scores by the number of scores in each condition.

Step 3: Compute the df_{AB} (multiply the number of levels of A – 1, times the number of levels of B – 1, and n – 1).

Step 4: Compute the MS_A (divide the SS_{AB} by the df_{AB}).

- How do the deviation scores used in the main effects of A and B compare with the steps used earlier for computing variance and standard deviation. What are the similarities and the differences?

Use the following formulae:

Computing the *F* ratios

Compare the main effect and interaction variance components with the variance within groups. For the main effect of A, divide the MS_A by the MS_{Within}. For the main effect of B, divide MS_B by the MS_{Within}. For the interaction of A and B, divide the MS_{AB} by the MS_{Within}.

- How are the three *F* ratios similar to each other? How are they different?

16F: MEET THE FORMULA AND PRACTICE PROBLEMS: ONE-FACTOR WITHIN-SUBJECTS ANALYSIS OF VARIANCE

Suppose that you want to see if there is an effect of an independent variable with three within-subjects levels. Consider the data that follows.

Group A	Group B	Group C
3	4	6
0	3	3
2	1	4
0	1	3
0	1	4

Here is the partitioning of the variance for this design that are needed to calculate the F ratio:

$$SS_{Between} = n \sum \left(\overline{X}_A - \overline{X}_{Grand} \right)^2 \qquad df_{Between} = a - 1 \qquad MS_{Between} = \frac{SS_{Between}}{df_{Between}}$$

$$SS_{Within} = n \sum \left(\overline{X}_{AB} - \overline{X}_A - \overline{X}_B + \overline{X}_{Grand} \right)^2 \qquad df_{Within} = a - 1 \qquad MS_{Within} = \frac{SS_{Within}}{df_{Within}}$$

$$F \ ratio = \frac{MS_{Between}}{MS_{Within}}$$

Recall that for a within-subjects design, there must be the same number of observations in each of the levels of the independent variable. This is because each participant experiences each condition of the study. In the df formula, a is the number of levels of the independent variable (in our example, we have three conditions).

1. Compare $SS_{Between}$ formulae for the one factor between-subjects ANOVA with the one-factor within-subjects ANOVA. Why can the n be moved outside of the summation in the between-groups variance formula for this data set?

    Recall that an interaction tells us if the differences across the levels of one factor are the same or different for each level of the other factor (i.e., Does the effect of one factor depend on the level of the other factor?). Here, one of our factors is the subjects, where each subject is a different level. We expect the subjects as a whole to differ across the conditions if the independent variable has an effect. But when the subjects show varying differences from one another across the conditions (i.e., an interaction between the subjects and the conditions), this represents the error we get from subject to subject in our study. Thus, we will use the interaction term as our error term because the interaction between subjects and the conditions will give us an estimate of the error that exists in our data based on differences from subject to subject across the conditions of the study.

2. Compare the within-groups variance formula for the within-subjects design with the between-groups variance formula for the interaction in the factorial between-subjects design. How do the formulae differ? Why are subjects considered a factor in the within-groups variance term for this design?

16G: MEET THE FORMULA AND PRACTICE PROBLEMS: CORRELATION

Computing the correlation between two continuous variables involves investigating how the scores on the two variables "move" relative to their standards and each other.

Here is the formula:

$$r = \frac{SP}{SS_X SS_Y} = \frac{\sum(X - \overline{X})(Y - \overline{Y})}{\sqrt{\sum(X - \overline{X})^2 \sum(Y - \overline{Y})^2}}$$

Using the formula:

Step 1: Compute the deviation scores for X and Y.

Step 2: Compute the sum of the products, multiply the deviation score of X and Y for each observation, and then add them all together.

Step 3: Compute the sum of the squared deviations (SS) for X and for Y. Add up all of the squared deviation scores for X, and then repeat for Y.

Step 4: Multiply the SS_X and SS_Y.

Step 5: Divide the sum of the products with the product of SS_X and SS_Y.

1. Consider the small data set that follows.

Person	X	Y
A	6	7
B	5	6
C	3	4
D	2	3
E	4	5

   a. Using the axes to the right of the table, make a scatterplot of X and Y. Based on your scatterplot, what value of r do you expect?

   b. Using the steps outlined previously, compute r.

   c. Examine the deviation scores that you used to compute the sum of products in the numerator. What do you notice about their signs (+ & −)?

2. Consider the small data set that follows.

Person	X	Y
A	6	4
B	5	3
C	3	1
D	4	2
E	7	5

a. Using the axes to the right of the table, make a scatterplot of X and Y. Based on your scatterplot, what value of r do you expect?

b. Using the steps outlined previously, compute r.

c. Examine the deviation scores that you used to compute the sum of products in the numerator. What do you notice about their signs (+ & –)?

d. What does a $r = -1.0$ (or $r = +1.0$) mean about the numerator and the denominator of the ratio? What does this suggest about how the covariance between X and Y compares with the product of how X and Y vary?

3. Consider the small data set that follows.

Person	X	Y
A	6	3
B	5	4
C	3	4
D	2	5

a. Make a scatterplot of X and Y. Based on your scatterplot, what value of r do you expect?

b. Imagine that the calculated r for this data set equaled 0. What value would you expect in the numerator of the formula for r with this result?

16H: MEET THE FORMULA AND PRACTICE PROBLEMS: BIVARIATE REGRESSION

Computing the components of bivariate regression share many similarities with the computations used for correlation. Scatterplots are useful graphs for visualizing both correlation and regression analyses. The regression analysis results in computing the slope and intercept of the "best fitting" line that characterizes the relationship between the two variables being compared.

Consider the small data set that follows.

Person	X	Y
A	6	7
B	5	6
C	3	4
D	2	3
E	4	5

1. Using the axes to the right of the table, make a scatterplot of X and Y. Draw a line through the points that you think fits best. Note where the line crosses the y-axis.

Regression	Correlation
$slope = b = \dfrac{SP}{SS_X} = \dfrac{\sum(X-\bar{X})(Y-\bar{Y})}{\sqrt{\sum(X-\bar{X})^2}}$	$r = \dfrac{SP}{SS_X SS_Y} = \dfrac{\sum(X-\bar{X})(Y-\bar{Y})}{\sqrt{(X-\bar{X})^2}}$
$intercept = a = \bar{Y} - b\bar{X}$	

a. Using the steps outlined before the table, compute the slope and intercept for the best fitting line. Plot that line on your scatterplot. How does it compare to your estimated line?

b. On your scatterplot, indicate a point that corresponds to X and Y. Does it fall on the line that you computed?

c. Examine the deviation scores that you used to compute the sum of products in the numerator in your slope computation. What do you notice about their signs (+ & −)?

d. Compare the formula for the slope with the formula for the correlation. How are they similar and different from each other?

APPENDIX A

Data Sets and Activities

A1. DATA ANALYSIS EXERCISE—VON HIPPEL, RONAY, BAKER, KJELSAAS, AND MURPHY (2016)

Use the following description of this study to conduct the appropriate data analysis and answer the following questions. Data are available for download from https://osf.io/dfm8r/.

Purpose of the Study. In this study, the researchers explored possible cognitive abilities that are related to social skills and one's charisma. In particular, they examined whether one's mental speed could predict social skills related to social comfort and conflict as well as interpreting others' feelings. They also tested whether one's mental speed could predict how charismatic, funny, and quick witted one was.

Method of the Study. Two studies were conducted. Each study included 200 participants that included groups of friends. In Study 1, participants completed an intelligence test (control measure), a five-factor personality survey (control measure), and 30 general knowledge questions (e.g., "Name a precious gem."). General knowledge questions provided the measure of mental speed, as participants were asked to answer the questions aloud as quickly as possible, and their time to answer was measured on each question. Participants also completed three-item surveys for both social skills and charisma, rating each person in their friend group on a 1 to 7 scale. In Study 2, the participants completed the same general knowledge questions, social skills and charisma ratings, and personality survey as in Study 1. In addition, participants in Study 2 also completed speeded left–right dot detection and pattern-matching tasks as measures of mental speed as well as surveys for self-control, self-efficacy (i.e., self-esteem), narcissism, social values, and self-confidence as control measures.

1. List any independent and dependent variables in these studies.

2. Were these studies experiments or correlational studies? Explain your answer.

3. Based on the stated purpose and the type of data collected, what is the appropriate statistical test for the data from these studies?

4. Download the data for the study, and conduct the hypothesis tests for Study 1 and Study 2. What conclusions should the authors have made from these results?

5. Download the article using the following reference. Take a look at the results for each study that correspond to the analyses you did (you can ignore other parts of their results that are more complicated and beyond the scope of this exercise). Did your results and conclusions match theirs? Why or why not?

von Hippel, W., Ronay, R., Baker, E., Kjelsaas, K., & Murphy, S. C. (2016). Quick thinkers are smooth talkers: Mental speed facilitates charisma. *Psychological Science, 27,* 119–122.

A2. DATA ANALYSIS EXERCISE—NAIRNE, PANDEIRADA, AND THOMPSON (2008)

Use the following description of this study to conduct the appropriate data analysis and answer the following questions. Data for the exercise are available for download from https://osf.io/4nd8g/.

Purpose of the Study. In this study, the researchers examined the effect of survival processing on later memory. They hypothesized that if information is processed according to its survival relevance when studied, that later memory for the information would be enhanced based on the adaptive value of memory.

Method of the Study. Participants were presented with words to rate one at a time. For some words, they rated the word's relevance to a survival scenario (S) if you were lost in the grasslands and had to find food, water, and shelter. For other words, they had to rate the word's relevance to going on vacation (V) to a fancy resort where you had to find activities to do and organize your time. Words were presented in blocks of eight words for each rating task, and each ratings task was presented twice. The order of the blocks was counterbalanced across participants (SVSV or VSVS). Ratings were made on a 1 to 5 scale, where higher ratings indicated higher relevance. After the fourth block of words, participants completed a short distractor task and then were given a surprise recall test for all of the words presented. The data file contains the counterbalancing condition, mean rating for each study task, mean percent recall of words for each study task, and the mean response time for rating the words for each study task for each participant.

1. List any independent and dependent variables in this study.

2. Was this study an experiment or correlational study? Explain your answer.

3. Based on the stated purpose and the type of data collected, what is the appropriate statistical test for the data from this study?

4. Download the data for the study, and conduct the hypothesis tests for this study. What conclusions should the authors have made from these results?

5. The data you analyzed are from the Reproducibility Project to replicate Experiment 2 of the Nairne et al. (2008) study. Download the article using the reference that follows. Take a look at the results for Experiment 2 from the article, and compare them to the analyses you did. Did your results and conclusions match theirs? Why or why not?

Nairne, J. S., Pandeirada, J. N. S., & Thompson, S. R. (2008). Adaptive memory: The comparative value of survival processing. *Psychological Science, 19*, 176–180.

A3. DATA ANALYSIS PROJECT—CRAMMED VS. DISTRIBUTED STUDY

Use the following description of this study and the data set indicated to answer the research questions listed. You will need to use both descriptive and inferential statistics to complete this project. You can download the SPSS data file Analysis_project_1.sav from **http://edge.sagepub .com/mcbridermstats1e** for the analyses. Write an American Psychological Association (APA)-style results section based on the analyses you conducted.

Research Project Description

The data for your project is the result of an organizational study of the effectiveness of a communication skill training program. Thirty management employees from the XYZ Corporation were interested in improving their group communication skills. These employees signed up for a 12-week "Group Communication and You" training course. An additional 30 management employees who were not interested in completing the training course served as a control or comparison group.

All employees were observed as they interacted in group settings prior to the training period. Observers recorded scores of employees' communication skills on a scale that ranged from 0 to 50 (with higher scores indicating better communication skills). After the 12-week training period (or, for the untrained group, after 12 weeks had passed), all employees were observed again and their communication effectiveness was rated using the same scale.

The researchers also measured employees' extraversion. Extraversion is defined as the extent to which individuals are outgoing, assertive, and sociable (high extraversion) versus reserved, timid, and quiet (low extraversion). This measure was given to all employees prior to the 12-week training period because the researchers suspected that extraversion may be related to one's communication effectiveness.

The researchers (pretend that's you) are interested in several things:

- Is there a difference in communication skills at Time2 between the trained and untrained groups?

- Did the trained group improve their communication skills after the training (Time 1 vs. Time 2)?

- Is extraversion related to communication skills?

Data Set Details

- *subject:* This refers to the subject number assigned to each subject. Each row corresponds to one subject's data.

- *traingp:* This variable refers to whether the employee is in the trained or untrained group: 0 = *untrained*, 1 = *trained*.

- *extrav:* This variable refers to the extraversion score of each subject.

- *time1:* This variable refers to the subjects' communication effectiveness scores prior to the 12-week period.

- *time2:* This variable refers to the subjects' communication effectiveness scores after the 12-week training period.

A4. DATA ANALYSIS PROJECT—TEACHING TECHNIQUES STUDY

Use the following description of this study and the data set indicated to answer the research questions listed. You will need to use both descriptive and inferential statistics to complete this project. You can download the SPSS data file Analysis_project_2.sav from **http://edge.sagepub .com/mcbridermstats1e** for the analyses. Write an APA-style results section based on the analyses you conducted.

Research Project Description

This study investigated the effect of teaching technique on measures of learning and interest in the topic. Two sections of a sociology course received different teaching formats. One section experienced a traditional lecture format, while the second section was taught with a combination of lectures, web-based activities, and in-class exercises. Learning of the course material was measured by the grade on the final exam, and interest was measured with a topical interest scale developed by the researcher.

The researchers (pretend that's you) are interested in several questions:

- Is there a difference between the two teaching formats in learning of the material?

- Is there a difference between the two teaching formats in interest in the material?

- Is learning related to interest in the topic?

Data Set Details

- *subject:* This refers to the subject number assigned to each subject. So each row corresponds to one subject's data.

- *teach:* This variable refers to which condition each subject was in: 1 = *lecture only*, 2 = *mixed*.

- *learn:* This variable refers to the learning of the material.

- *interest:* This variable refers to the interest in the topic.

A5. DATA ANALYSIS PROJECT—DISTRACTED DRIVING STUDY

Use the following description of this study and the data set indicated to answer the research questions listed. You will need to use both descriptive and inferential statistics to complete this project. You can download the SPSS data file Analysis_project_3.sav from **http://edge.sagepub.com/mcbridermstats1e** for the analyses. Write an APA-style results section based on the analyses you conducted.

Research Project Description

This study investigated the effects of distractions while driving. Participants were asked to drive a car around a test track of orange cones. Two types of distracting activities were tested: one group of drivers conducted a conversation on a cell phone while driving the course, and the other group were asked to eat a Big Mac Extra Value Meal (Big Mac, fries, and a drink) while driving the course. Both the average driving speed and the number of orange cones knocked over were measured.

The researchers (pretend that's you) are interested in several questions:

- Is there a difference between eating talking on a cell phone for average speed?

- Is there a difference between eating talking on a cell phone for number of cones knocked over?

- Is average speed related to number of cones knocked down?

Data Set Details

- *subject:* This refers to the subject number assigned to each subject. Each row corresponds to one subject's data.

- distrac*:* This variable refers to which condition each subject was in: 1 = *eating*, 2 = *cell phone*.

- *speed:* This variable refers to the average driving speed.

- *cones:* This variable refers to the total number of cones knocked over.

A6. DATA ANALYSIS PROJECT—TEMPERATURE AND AIR QUALITY STUDY

Use the following description of this study and the data set indicated to answer the research questions listed. You will need to use both descriptive and inferential statistics to complete this project. You can download the SPSS data file Analysis_project_4.sav from **http://edge.sagepub .com/mcbridermstats1e** for the analyses. Write an APA-style results section based on the analyses you conducted.

Research Project Description

The Environmental Protection Agency is investigating claims that global temperatures are higher and air quality is worse now than they were in 1950. They sample the temperature on a single day in several random cities. They also measure the air quality index for these cities. Data were collected in a similar manner from random cities in 1950.

The researchers (pretend that's you) are interested in several questions:

- Is there a difference between 1950 and 2003 temperatures?

- Is there a difference between 1950 and 2003 air quality?

- Is temperature related to air quality?

Data Set Details

- *city:* This refers to the subject number assigned to each city. Each row corresponds to one city's data.

- *year:* This variable refers to which condition each subject was in: 1 = *1950*, 2 = *2003*.

- *temp:* This variable refers to the temperature in the city when sampled.

- *quality:* This variable refers to the air quality in the city when sampled (higher scores mean better air).

A7. DATA ANALYSIS PROJECT—JOB TYPE AND SATISFACTION STUDY

Use the following description of this study and the data set indicated to answer the research questions listed. You will need to use both descriptive and inferential statistics to complete this project. You can download the SPSS data file Analysis_project_5.sav from **http://edge.sagepub .com/mcbridermstats1e** for the analyses. Write an APA-style results section based on the analyses you conducted.

Research Project Description

This study examined the effect of job type (or status) on job satisfaction. Researchers studied two types of job satisfaction (specifically, satisfaction with pay and satisfaction with the work itself) among a group of university faculty and staff. Each group completed a questionnaire measuring their satisfaction with work and satisfaction with pay.

The researchers (pretend that's you) are interested in several questions:

- Is there a difference between faculty and staff in satisfaction with pay?

- Is there a difference between faculty and staff in satisfaction with work itself?

- Is satisfaction with work related to satisfaction with pay?

Data Set Details

- *subject:* This refers to the subject number assigned to each subject. Each row corresponds to one subject's data

- *status:* This variable refers to which condition each subject was in: 1 = *faculty*, 2 = *staff*.

- *pay:* This variable refers to the satisfaction with pay measure.

- *work:* This variable refers to the satisfaction with work measure.

A8. DATA ANALYSIS PROJECT—ATTRACTIVE FACE RECOGNITION STUDY

Use the following description of this study and the data set indicated to answer the research questions listed. You will need to use both descriptive and inferential statistics to complete this project. You can download the SPSS file Analysis_project_6.sav from **http://edge.sagepub.com/ mcbridermstats1e** for the analyses. Write an APA-style results section based on the analyses you conducted.

Research Project Description

This study investigated the effects of previous exposure on perceived physical attractiveness. In the first phase of the experiment, all of the participants were presented 100 photographs of faces on a computer screen and asked to make an age estimation of each (e.g., How old do you think this person is?). In the second phase of the experiment, participants were again presented with photos of faces and asked to make two judgments: the attractiveness of this person (scale of 1 [*unattractive*] to 7 [*very attractive*]) and the familiarity of this person (1 [*not familiar*] to 7 [*very familiar*]). For one group of participants, 10 of the photos were from the original list (plus there were 15 photos of celebrities and 15 unemployed actors, but these photos were just filler pictures and not used in the analysis of the data). For another group of participants, there were 10 photos of new faces (plus the filler pictures).

The researchers (pretend that's you) are interested in several questions:

- Is there a difference in perceived attractiveness between the photos from the original list and the 10 new photos?

- Is there a difference in familiarity between the photos from the original list and the 10 new photos?

- Is attractiveness related to familiarity?

Data Set Details

- *subject:* This refers to the subject number assigned to each subject. Each row corresponds to one subject's data.

- *faces:* This variable refers to which condition each subject was in: 1 = *new faces*, 2 = *old faces*.

- *attract:* This variable refers to the average rated attractiveness.

- *famil:* This variable refers to the average rated familiarity.

A9. DATA ANALYSIS PROJECT—DISCRIMINATION IN THE WORKPLACE STUDY

Use the following description of this study and the data set indicated to answer the research questions listed. You will need to use both descriptive and inferential statistics to complete this project. You can download the SPSS data file Analysis_project_7.sav from **http://edge.sagepub .com/mcbridermstats1e** for the analyses. Write an APA-style results section based on the analyses you conducted.

Research Project Description

This study investigated occurrences of discrimination in the workplace. In two different years (2014 and 2016), employees at a company were asked to report the number of incidents of discrimination they experienced at work. In the year between (2015), some employees participated in a discrimination awareness workshop. Different levels of employees were included in the study. Other demographics variables were also measured.

The researchers (pretend that's you) are interested in several questions:

- What do the distributions of discrimination reports look like across years? Describe the distributions for discrimination in both 2014 and 2016.

- Which variables are significantly correlated with one another? Describe these relationships.

- Is there a significant change in discrimination reports from 2014 to 2016?

- Is there a significant change in discrimination reports in 2016 depending on training program?

- Is there an effect of job level on discrimination reports in 2016? Using a Tukey test, which groups are statistically different?

- Is there a significant interaction of gender and workshop participation on discrimination reports in 2016? If so, describe the interaction.

Data Set Details

- Participation: Some employees chose to attend the discrimination awareness workshop (1 = *participated*, 2 = *did not participate*) in 2015

- Gender: 1 = *female*, 2 = *male*

- Age: Age of employee at 2016 testing

- Joblevel: 1 = *staff*, 2 = *lower management*, 3 = *upper management*

- Yearscom: Number of years employed at the company at 2016 testing

- Yearsed: Number of years of post-high school education

- Jobsat: Job satisfaction score from questionnaire (higher scores mean greater satisfaction)

- Ethnicity: Self-reported ethnicity

- Discr2014: Number of discrimination incidents reported during the past year (2014)

- Discr2016: Number of discrimination incidents reported during the past year (2016)

APPENDIX B

Overview and Selection of Statistical Tests

B1: FINDING THE APPROPRIATE INFERENTIAL TEST

Use the flowchart to answer the questions about the correct statistical test for each situation described. Indicate if there is more than one appropriate test and in which cases each test should be used.

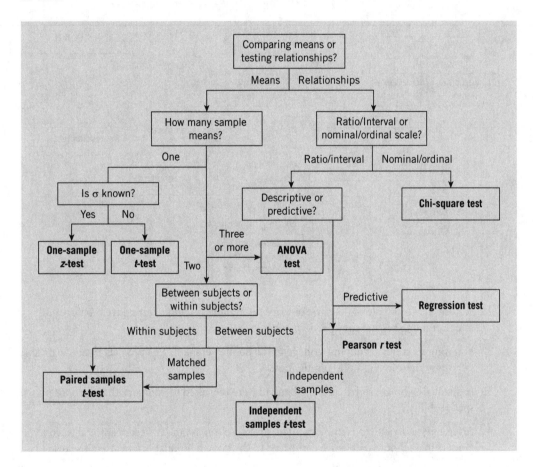

1. You want to describe the relationship between two measured variables.

2. You have a single sample that you want to compare with a population with a known mean (μ).

3. You have two sample means (from different groups of subjects) that you want to compare.

4. You want to be able to predict a score on a ratio variable from a score on an interval variable.

5. You have sets of twins you are comparing on a measure.

B2: FINDING THE APPROPRIATE INFERENTIAL TEST FROM RESEARCH DESIGNS

Use the flowchart to answer the questions about the correct statistical test for each situation described. Indicate if there is more than one appropriate test and in which cases each test should be used.

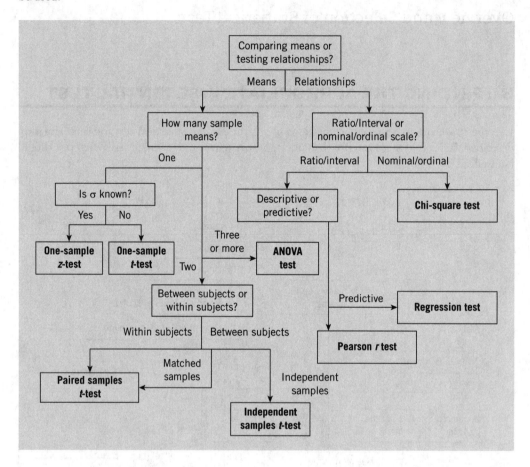

1. A study uses a sample of dogs to compare their ability to find a buried treat before and after a training session they participate in.

2. You want to know if students' college grade point average (GPA) predicts their starting salaries in their first job post-graduation.

3. Individuals who are right- and left-handed were recruited to compare these groups on spatial ability.

4. After a new curriculum is implemented, the scores on a standardized test for all second graders in a school ($n = 80$) are compared to the known population mean on the test.

5. You want to know how studying with silence, classical, or rock music in the background compare in terms of exam scores for a class.

B3: FINDING THE APPROPRIATE INFERENTIAL TEST FROM RESEARCH QUESTIONS

For the research questions that follow, describe a study to answer the question using the research design specified. Be sure to state any dependent variables in your study. State your hypothesis for your study, and use the flowchart to indicate which statistical test(s) you could use to test your hypothesis.

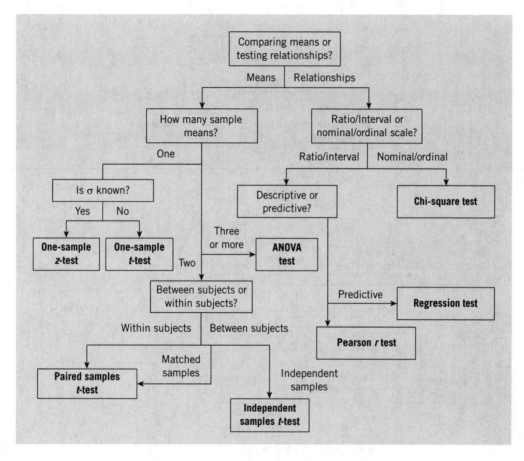

1. Does watching violence on TV cause violent behavior? (experiment)

2. Do people who play video games have better hand–eye coordination in other tasks? (correlational)

3. Does divorce in families negatively affect children? (correlational)

4. Are smoking and lung cancer related? (quasi-experiment)

5. Does studying with background music improve test scores? (experiment)

6. Are there fewer helping behaviors in large cities? (correlational)

7. Are color and mood related? (correlational)

8. Are caffeine and work productivity related? (quasi-experiment)

9. Does watching violence on TV cause violent behavior? (correlational)

10. Do people who play video games have better hand–eye coordination in other tasks? (experiment)

B4: IDENTIFYING THE DESIGN AND FINDING THE APPROPRIATE INFERENTIAL TEST FROM ABSTRACTS

For each study description that follows, identify the data collection technique and the research design that were used. Then use the flowchart to indicate which inferential test should be used to analyze the data for that study.

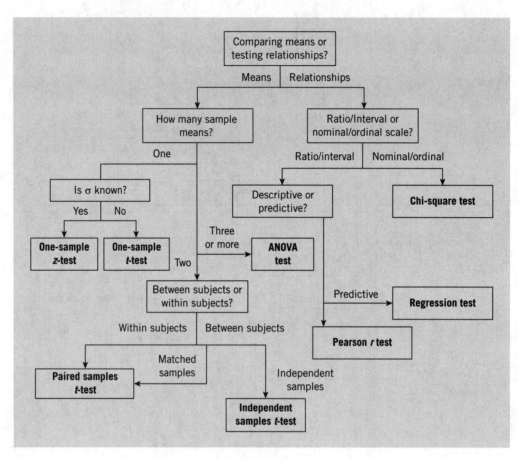

1. Researchers (Bartecchi et al., 2006) were interested in the effects of a new law banning smoking in public places on health. They compared heart attack rates for two cities of comparable size where one city had enacted a smoking ban 1 year before the study and the other city had no smoking ban. To compare heart attack rates, the researchers examine hospital records for the hospitals in each city. They compared heart attack rates for the year before the smoking ban in each city and for the year after the ban was enacted. They found that heart attack rates decreased in the city with ban from one year to the next, but did not decrease in the city without the ban.

Data Collection Technique:

Research Design:

Statistical Test:

2. To evaluate the validity of a newly created survey measure of college students' satisfaction with their major, a researcher (Nauta, 2007) administered the survey to college students who had declared a major. She then also collected the students' GPAs (with their permission) from the university registrar to examine the relationship between their survey score and their GPA. She found that satisfaction with major was positively correlated with GPA.

Data Collection Techniques (There is more than one in this study.):

Research Design:

Statistical Test:

What does it mean that she found a positive relationship between GPA and survey score?

3. Researchers (Assefi & Garry, 2003) were interested in the effects of the belief that one has consumed alcohol on cognition. In particular, they tested whether a belief that subjects had consumed alcohol during the study would increase their susceptibility to memory errors. Subjects were randomly assigned to one of two groups. In one group, they were told the drink they consumed had contained alcohol (with some alcohol rubbed on the outside of the glass for realism). In the other group, they were told the drink did not contain alcohol. All subjects then saw a slide show of a crime (shoplifting). After a short delay, subjects then read a description of the crime that contained errors. After another short delay, they answered questions about the slides they had seen and were asked to rate their confidence in their answers. Subjects told they drank alcohol made more errors in their answers and were more confident in their responses.

Data Collection Technique:

Research Design:

Statistical Test:

B5: IDENTIFYING VARIABLES AND DETERMINING THE INFERENTIAL TEST FROM ABSTRACTS

For each study description that follows, list the relevant variables, and then use the flowchart to find the correct statistical test to use and which effects will be tested in this analysis.

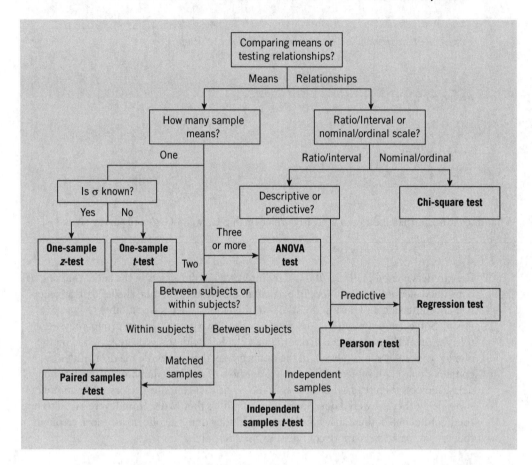

1. A psychologist is interested in the effect of peer pressure on risk-taking behaviors of college students. The psychologist designs an experiment to determine this effect wherein 200 students (who volunteer to serve as participants) are randomly placed in one of two situations. In each situation, five participants sit in a room with four other people. The four other people are actually confederates of the experimenter (i.e., they are part of the experiment), and their behavior is determined before the experiment begins. Half of the participants witness the four other people in the room leaning back in their chairs (a behavior that involves the minor risk of falling over backward in the chair). The other half of the participants also witness the four confederates leaning back in their chairs but are further encouraged by the confederates to exhibit the same behavior (e.g., they tell the subjects that leaning back is more comfortable, fun). The behavior of each participant is observed to determine if they do or do not lean back in their chair during the experiment. For each group, the number of participants (out of five) who lean back in their chairs is recorded.

   a. List any independent variables in this study and the levels of each one.

   b. What is the dependent variable, and how is it being measured?

   c. What statistical test should be used to analyze the data from this experiment? What effects will be tested in this analysis?

2. A research methods instructor wants to know if having students conduct their own research study as part of the course increases their understanding of major concepts in the course. To investigate this, she gives two sections of her course a pretest on the course concepts. She then gives one section a research study assignment for the course but does not give this assignment to her other section. At the end of the semester, she gives a posttest to both sections on the course concepts and compares the difference in the pretest–posttest scores as a measure of learning for the two sections of her course. The section with the research study assignment shows more learning.

   a. List the quasi-independent variables in this study and the levels of each one.

   b. What is the dependent variable, and how is it being measured?

   c. What statistical test should be used to analyze the data from this quasi-experiment? What effects will be tested in this analysis?

APPENDIX C

Summary of Formulae

Descriptive statistics	For a population	For a sample
Mean	$\mu = \sum \dfrac{X}{n}$	$\overline{X} = \sum \dfrac{X}{n}$
Sum of squares	$SS = \sum (X - \mu)^2$	$SS = \sum \left(X - \overline{X}\right)^2$
Variance	$\sigma^2 = \dfrac{SS}{N}$	$s^2 = \dfrac{SS}{n-1}$
Standard deviation	$\sigma = \sqrt{\sigma^2} = \sqrt{\dfrac{SS}{N}}$	$s = \sqrt{s^2} = \sqrt{\dfrac{SS}{n-1}}$
Z score	$z = \dfrac{X - \mu}{\sigma}$	$z = \dfrac{X - \overline{X}}{s}$

Correlation and Regression Statistics

Sum of the products: $SP = \sum \left(X - \overline{X}\right)\left(Y - \overline{Y}\right)$

Pearson's correlation coefficient: $r = \dfrac{SP}{\sqrt{SS_X SS_Y}}$ $\quad r = \dfrac{\sum z_X z_Y}{n-1}$

Degrees of freedom: $df = n - 2$

Regression line: $\hat{Y} = (X)(\text{slope}) + (\text{intercept}) = Xb + a = bX + a$

Slope: $b = \dfrac{SP}{SS_X}$

Intercept: $a = \overline{Y} - b\overline{X}$

Total squared error: $SS = \left(Y - \hat{Y}\right)^2$

Standard error of estimate: $s_{est} = \sqrt{\dfrac{SS_{error}}{df}}$

Hypothesis Testing and Parameter Estimation

z Test

Standard error (σ known): $\sigma_{\overline{X}} = \dfrac{\sigma}{\sqrt{n}}$

z observed: $z_{\overline{X}} = \dfrac{\overline{X} - \mu}{\sigma_{\overline{X}}}$

Effect size: $d = \dfrac{\overline{X} - \mu}{\sigma}$

Parameter estimate (σ known): $\mu = \overline{X} \pm z_{\text{crit}}(\sigma_{\overline{X}})$

One-Sample t Test

Degrees of freedom: $n - 1$

Standard error (σ unknown): $s_{\overline{X}} = \dfrac{s}{\sqrt{n}}$

One-sample t observed: $t = \dfrac{\overline{X} - \mu}{s_{\overline{X}}}$

Effect size: $d = \dfrac{\overline{X} - \mu}{s}$

Parameter estimate (σ unknown): $\mu = \overline{X} \pm t_{\text{crit}}\left(s_{\overline{X}}\right)$

Related-Samples t Test

Degrees of freedom: $n_{D} - 1$

Mean of differences: $\overline{D} = \dfrac{\sum D}{n}$

Sum of squares of differences: $SS_D \sum \left(D - \overline{D}\right)^2$

Standard deviation of differences: $s_D = \sqrt{\dfrac{SS_D}{n_D - 1}} = \sqrt{\dfrac{\left(D - \overline{D}\right)^2}{n_D - 1}}$

Standard error of differences: $s_{\overline{D}} = \dfrac{s_D}{\sqrt{n_D}}$

Related-samples t observed: $t_D = \dfrac{\overline{D} - \mu_D}{s_D}$

Effect size: $d = \dfrac{\overline{D}}{s_D}$

Parameter estimate (related samples): $\mu_D = \overline{D} \pm t_{\text{crit}}\left(s_{\overline{D}}\right)$

Independent-Samples t Test

Degrees of freedom: $df_1 = (n_1 - 1), df_2 = (n_2 - 1)$

$df_{\text{total}} = df_1 + df_2 = n_1 + n_2 - 2$

Pooled variance of independent samples: $s_p^2 = \dfrac{SS_1 + SS_2}{df_1 + df_2}$ $s_p^2 = \dfrac{s_1^2 + s_2^2}{2}$
(2nd averaging formulas if $n_1 = n_2$)

Standard error of independent samples: $s_{(\overline{X}_1 - \overline{X}_2)} = \sqrt{\dfrac{s_p^2}{n_1} + \dfrac{s_p^2}{n_2}}$ $s_{(\overline{X}_1 - \overline{X}_2)} = \sqrt{\dfrac{2s_p^2}{n}} = s_p \sqrt{\dfrac{2}{n}}$
(2nd formula if $n_1 = n_2$)

Independent-samples observed t: $t_{obs} = \dfrac{(\overline{X}_1 - \overline{X}_2) - (\mu_1 - \mu_2)}{s_{(\overline{X} - \overline{X}_2)}}$

Effect size: $d = \dfrac{\overline{X}_2 - \overline{X}_1}{s_p}$

Parameter (independent samples): $\mu_1 - \mu_2 = \overline{X}_1 - \overline{X}_2 \pm t_{crit}\left(s_{(X_1 - X_2)}\right)$

Chi-Square Test

Estimated cell frequencies: $f_e = \dfrac{f_{column} f_{row}}{n}$ or $f_e = \dfrac{f_{row}}{n} * f_{column}$

Observed chi-square: $\chi^2 = \sum \dfrac{(f_o - f_e)^2}{f_e}$

Degrees of freedom: $df = (\#columns - 1)*(\#rows - 1)$

One-Factor Between-Subjects Analysis of Variance (ANOVA)

$SS_{Total} = \sum \left(X - \overline{X}_{Grand}\right)^2$ $df_{Total} = N - 1$ $MS_{Total} = \dfrac{SS_{Total}}{df_{Total}}$

One-Factor Within-Subjects ANOVA

$SS_{Between} = n \sum \left(\overline{X}_A - \overline{X}_{Grand}\right)^2$ $df_{Between} = a - 1$ $MS_{Between} = \dfrac{SS_{Between}}{df_{Between}}$

$SS_{Within} = n \sum \left(\overline{X}_{AB} - \overline{X}_A - \overline{X}_B + \overline{X}_{Grand}\right)^2$ $df_{Within} = a - 1$ $MS_{Within} = \dfrac{SS_{Within}}{df_{Within}}$

$F - ratio = \dfrac{MS_{Between}}{MS_{Within}}$

Two-Factor ANOVA

$SS_{Total} = \sum \left(X - \overline{X}_{Grand}\right)^2$ $df_{Total} = N - 1$ $MS_{Total} = \dfrac{SS_{Total}}{df_{Total}}$

$SS_{Within} = \sum \left(X - \overline{X}_{AB}\right)^2$ $df_{within} = (a)*(b)(n-1)$ $MS_{Within} = \dfrac{SS_{Within}}{df_{Within}}$

$SS_A = n(b) \sum \left(\overline{X}_A - \overline{X}_{Grand}\right)^2$ $df_A = a - 1$ $MS_A = \dfrac{SS_{Within}}{df_{Within}}$

$SS_B = n(a) \sum \left(\overline{X}_B - \overline{X}_{Grand}\right)^2$ $df_B = b - 1$ $MS_A = \dfrac{SS_{Within}}{df_{Within}}$

$df_{AB} = (a)*(b)(n-1)$ $MS_{AB} = \dfrac{SS_{within}}{df_{within}}$ $MS_B = \dfrac{SS_{within}}{df_{within}}$

$SS_{AB} = n \sum \left(\overline{X}_{AB} - \overline{X}_{AB} - \overline{X}_B + \overline{X}_{Grand}\right)^2$

REFERENCES

Abel, M., & Roediger, H. L., III (2018). The testing effect in a social setting: Does retrieval practice benefit a listener? *Journal of Experimental Psychology: Applied*, 24(3), 347–359.

Assefi, S. L., & Garry, M. (2003). Absolut memory distortions: Alcohol placebos influence the misinformation effect. *Psychological Science*, 14, 77–80.

Axt, J. R. (2018). The best way to measure explicit racial attitudes is to ask about them. *Social Psychological and Personality Science*, 9(8), 896–906.

Bartecchi, C., Alsever, R. N., Nevin-Woods, C., Thomas, W. M., Estacio, R. O., Bartelson, B. B., & Krantz, M. J. (2006). Reduction in the incidence of acute myocardial infarction associated with a city-wide smoking ordinance. *Circulation*, 114, 1490–1496.

Braun, K. A., & Loftus, E. F. (1998). Advertising's misinformation effect. *Applied Cognitive Psychology*, 12, 569–591.

Cantlon, J. F., & Brannon, E. M. (2006). Shared system for ordering small and large numbers in monkeys and humans. *Psychological Science*, 17, 401–406.

Chartrand, T. L., & Bargh, J. A. (1999). The chameleon effect: The perception–behavior link and social interaction. *Journal of Personality and Social Psychology*, 76, 893–910.

Farmer, H., McKay, R., & Tsakiris, M. (2014). Trust in me: Trustworthy others are seen as more physically similar to the self. *Psychological Science*, 25, 290–292.

Farooqui, A. A., & Manly, T. (2015). Anticipatory control through associative learning of subliminal relations: Invisible may be better than visible. *Psychological Science*, 26, 325–334.

Jackson, J. J., Connolly, J. J., Garrison, S. M., Leveille, M. M., & Connolly, S. L. (2015). Your friends know how long you will live: A 75-year study of peer-rated personality traits. *Psychological Science*, 26, 335–340.

Jirout, J. J., & Newcombe, N. S. (2015). Building blocks for developing spatial skills: Evidence from a large, representative U.S. sample. *Psychological Science*, 26, 302–310.

Lane, L. W., Groisman, M., & Ferreira, V. S. (2006). Don't talk about pink elephants! Speakers' control over leaking private information during language production. *Psychological Science*, 17, 273–277.

Mueller, P. A., & Oppenheimer, D. M. (2014). The pen is mightier than the keyboard: Advantages of longhand over laptop notetaking. *Psychological Science*, 25, 1159–1168.

Nairne, J. S., Pandeirada, J. N. S., & Thompson, S. R. (2008). Adaptive memory: The comparative value of survival processing. *Psychological Science*, 19, 176–180.

Nauta, M. M. (2007). Assessing college students' satisfaction with their academic majors. *Journal of Career Assessment*, 15, 446–462.

Roediger, H. L., III, & Karpicke, J. D. (2006). Test-enhanced learning: Taking memory tests improves long-term retention. *Psychological Science*, 17, 249–255.

Sayette, M. A., Reichle, E. D., & Schooler, J. W. (2009). Lost in the sauce: The effects of alcohol on mind wandering. *Psychological Science*, 20, 747–752.

Sproesser, G., Schupp, H. T., & Renner, B. (2014). The bright side of stress-induced eating: Eating more when stressed but less when pleased. *Psychological Science*, 25, 58–65.

Stanley, M. L., Henne, P., & De Brigard, F. (in press). Remembering moral and immoral actions in constructing the self. *Memory and Cognition*.

Tsapelas, I., Aron, A., & Orbuch, T. (2009). Marital boredom now predicts less satisfaction 9 years later. *Psychological Science*, 20, 543–545.

Vohs, K. D., & Schooler, J. W. (2008). The value of believing in free will. *Psychological Science*, 19, 49–54.

von Hippel, W., Ronay, R., Baker, E., Kjelsaas, K., & Murphy, S. C. (2016). Quick thinkers are smooth talkers: Mental speed facilitates charisma. *Psychological Science*, 27, 119–122. doi:10.1177/0956797615616255